# Somerset & Dorset Demise

### Jeffery Grayer

TURNTABLE PUBLISHING

# Somerset & Dorset Demise

© Design: The Transport Treasury 2021. Images as credited. Uncredited images are by the Author.

ISBN 978-1-915281-00-5

First Published in 2021 by Transport Treasury Publishing Ltd.,
Turntable Publishing, an imprint of Transport Treasury Publishing.
16 Highworth Close, High Wycombe, HP13 7PJ

www.ttpublishing.co.uk

Printed in Tarxien, Malta by Gutenberg Press Ltd.

The copyright holders hereby give notice that all rights to this work are reserved. Aside from brief passages for the purpose of review, no part of this work may be reproduced, copied by electronic or other means, or otherwise stored in any information storage and retrieval system without written permission from the Publisher.

This includes the illustrations herein which remain the copyright of the respective copyright holder.

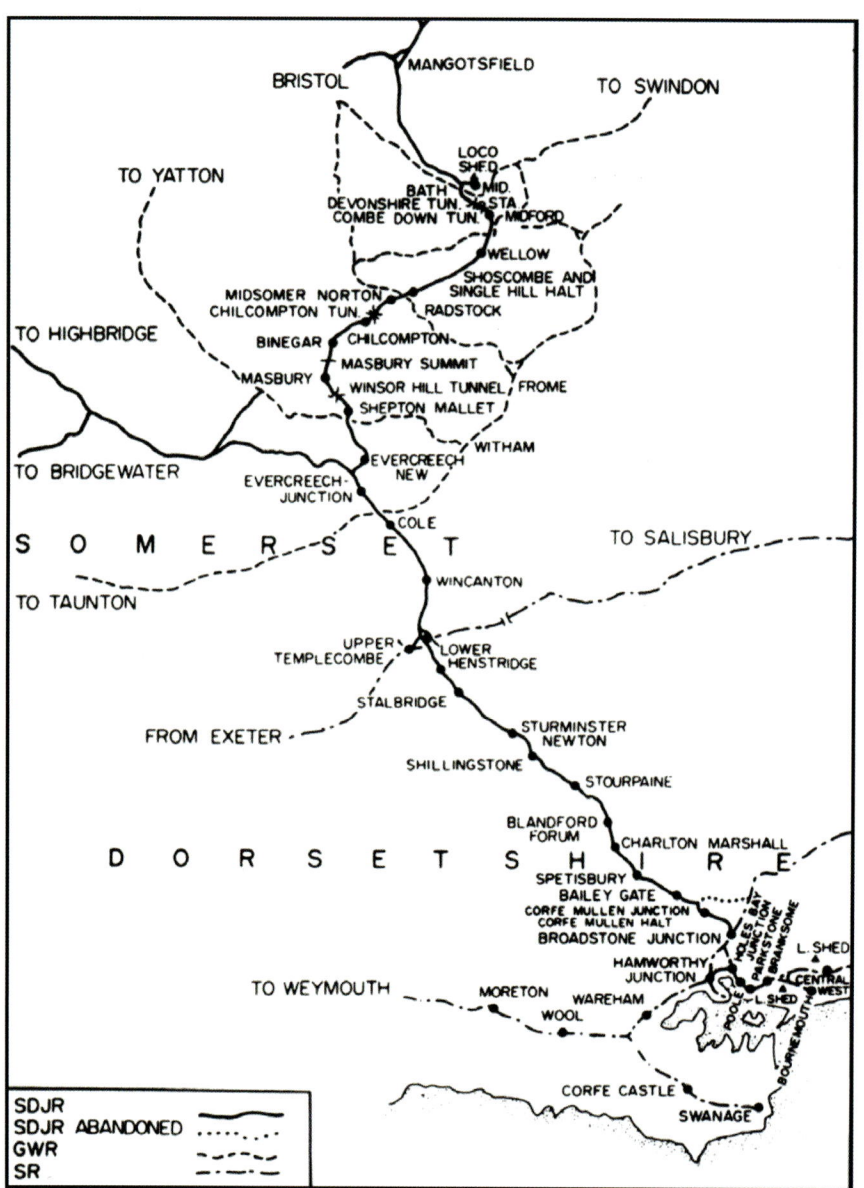

**Front Cover:** A pair of "bulled up" Bulleids captured at rest on Green Park shed on the afternoon of Saturday 5th. March 1966, the final day of public services, prior to returning south with the LCGB "Somerset & Dorset Railtour". This pairing provided a fitting epitaph to services over the line as these pacifics had been a feature of the motive power on the line since they first appeared back in 1951. *Mark Warburton courtesy Mrs M Warburton*

**Frontispiece:** A demolition train hauling wagons loaded with recovered track materials from the railhead near Shillingstone arrives at the former down platform at Evercreech Junction on 15th. May 1967 with North British Type 2 locomotive No. D6331 at its head. At the Junction crews would be exchanged with the southbound recovery train headed by a Bristol crew. The Yeovil based crew would then return south to the railhead with the empty wagons ready to receive further recovered materials. *Derek Fear*

**Rear Cover:** As Private Frazer of "Dad's Army" might have said – "Aye Masbury, 'tis a wild and lonely place"... although in this summertime view the scene is somewhat more benevolent. The signalbox has lost its nameboard indicating that this shot probably dates from the summer of 1964, after closure of the box on 1st. July but prior to demolition which occurred shortly afterwards. *Graham Smith courtesy Richard Simmons*

## Contents

| | |
|---|---|
| 1 Introduction | 4 |
| 2 The writing on the wall (pre 1965) | 5 |
| 3 On borrowed time (1965 - final full year of operations,) | 14 |
| 4 Last gasp (1966) | 67 |
| 5 Aftermath (1966 - 1980) | 86 |
| 6 Erasing the past | 108 |

In the teeth of a strong cross wind, which snatches away the exhaust of Standard Class 4 2-6-0 No. 76009, the 13:10 stopping service from Bath to Templecombe powers up the gradient on the approach to the summit at Masbury on 1st. December 1965. This was to be the final month of anything like a full service before the introduction of the "Emergency" timetable the following month. *Derek Fear*

# Introduction

The takeover of the northern half of the Somerset & Dorset line by the Western Region in 1958 together with the re-routing of through services away from the line at the end of the summer service in 1962 were to have significant implications for the future of this long cross country route. It could never survive as an expensive steam operated line with the purely local traffic offering and against a background of the swingeing Beeching cuts of the early 1960s and the lack of investment its fate was sealed. It was expected that closure would come in January 1966 however, as is well known, closure was postponed until March due to the inability of one of the bus operators to provide a rail replacement service necessitating the implementation of an "Emergency" rail service for a few weeks until closure could finally be effected on 6th. March 1966.

In this volume we take a brief look at the years from 1962 onwards beginning with the final summer of through expresses in 1962 often hauled by Standard 9Fs and continue into 1965 the final full year of services when three or four coach locals constituted the norm. We then cover 1966 leading to the final few enthusiast specials run to mark the closure in March. Some of the few remaining freight services operating over isolated truncated portions of the route and the operation of demolition trains which assisted in the task of taking up the track are also covered as is the aftermath during which much of the route's infrastructure was inexorably destroyed. The last trio of remaining collieries operating in the North Somerset coalfield is also featured as are subsequent specials that ventured as far as Radstock and Blandford Forum.

As the author of six previous books on the line, two of which are now out of print, I would like to thank Transport Treasury for this opportunity to round off the story and to pay tribute once again to the foresight of ex railwayman Derek Fear who, recognising that the end was near, began to take colour slides covering the dying days of the line from 1965 onwards together with the sad aftermath. Fortunately he also recorded locomotive numbers and train details so that we are able to identify the workings pictured. None of his slides featured here have been published before. I would also like to thank photographers Geoff Plumb and George Woods some of whose collection I have used in previous volumes and thanks also go to the S&D Railway Trust (S&DRT) whose collection of stunning images has provided a further source of colour material which becomes ever more elusive with the passing years. Although this volume has been published in 2021, to mark the 55th. anniversary of the closure of the line, the passage of the intervening decades does not appear to have diminished the continuing level of interest in this fascinating route.

*Jeffery Grayer*

*Devon, 2021*

**Left:** Situated next to bridge No. 243 at Pylle station this S&DJR notice, signed by the Joint Secretaries of the LMS and LSWR and dated 9th. August 1903 and carrying a dire warning of a penalty of 40/- for trespassing, was photographed on 12th. October 1965. The bridge was demolished in 1970 by Somerset County Council for road improvements. *Derek Fear*

**Opposite top:** Our earliest view is of 7F No. 53808 which has charge of the 07:35 from Nottingham to Bournemouth service seen here at Evercreech Junction on Saturday 4th August 1962. Although essentially freight locomotives these 2-8-0s were often pressed into service to handle some of the summer Saturday through trains. No doubt after a journey of many hours residents of Nottinghamshire would be glad to reach their seaside destination. *S&DRT*

# 2
# The writing on the wall (pre 1965)

**Above:** No. 75027 on the 11:12 Bournemouth to Sheffield service is captured rumbling over the A371 level crossing prior to its stop at Evercreech Junction also on Saturday 4th August 1962. Having left Bournemouth at 09:45 Sheffield would not be reached until almost seven hours later at 16:40. 1962 would be the final summer of through services over the S&D to the Midlands and the North of England, a decision which would ultimately contribute to the demise of the route. *S&DRT*

# The writing on the wall

Opposite: Shoscombe & Single Hill Halt hosts the 16:15 Templecombe - Bath service powered by 4F No. 44102 on Saturday 25th. August 1962. The guard waves his green flag to signal "right away" for the 21 minute journey into Bath. The inhabitants of this hamlet poorly served by public transport today would I am sure welcome back the trains with open arms. Staffing throughout the existence of the halt was in the hands of two sisters – the Misses Tapper later Mrs Beeho and Mrs Chivers – who were apparently always ready for a gossip in the booking office which they ran like a community centre. It was all part of a friendly little railway which had a strong sense of belonging amongst its staff and which was valued and appreciated by regular travellers. *S&DRT*

Above: Although station staff were not withdrawn from Midford until February 1964 one of the regular signalmen, Harry Wiltshire, can be seen lending a hand by wielding a brush in an attempt to keep the platform shipshape. Great pride was taken in maintaining the sparkling condition of the signalbox until the very last day and this ethic obviously extended to the whole station. If the timetable advertised on one of the poster boards is current then this dates this shot to between June and September 1963. One of the line's famous "backing signals" is very evident. *Wilf Stanley*

## Somerset & Dorset Demise

Above: This detailed view of Radstock North 'B' signalbox dates from the summer of 1962 and was taken from Waterloo Road. The signalman can be seen taking a breather whilst the large BR poster board on the right extols the virtues of domestic travel to London, Poole and Bournemouth. The advantages of dispatching through wagons by train ferry to the Continent are also advertised. The entrance to the subway beneath the signalbox can also be seen which enabled pedestrians and the smallest of cars to avoid queuing at the level crossing gates although in times of heavy rain it was subject to flooding. *S&DRT*

Opposite top: Ex-GWR Collett No. 3215 has arrived at Evercreech Junction with a service from Highbridge on the 8th. September 1962. The first of several members of this class of 0-6-0 was drafted onto the S&D in April 1960 with No. 3215 being the second to be allocated to Templecombe shed in June 1960 where it lasted in service until withdrawal in January 1963. Another locomotive has coupled to the rear of the train to retrieve the four coaches from the down platform ready to position them for their next trip up the branch. By the latter days of the branch the four coach train seen here had reduced to just one coach and van reflecting the declining level of patronage. *Douglas Twiball*

Opposite bottom: No. 92224 seen here after arrival at Templecombe was drafted in to assist with Green Park's motive power shortage for a couple of months in the summer of 1963. In the absence of any through expresses to haul it was reduced to lowly duties such as this one hauling a couple of cattle wagons and a short rake of coaches. The 12th. century church of St. Mary, whose sonorous bell chimes regularly punctuated the silence on Templecombe's platforms, can be seen on the left. *Graham Smith courtesy Richard Sissons*

# The writing on the wall

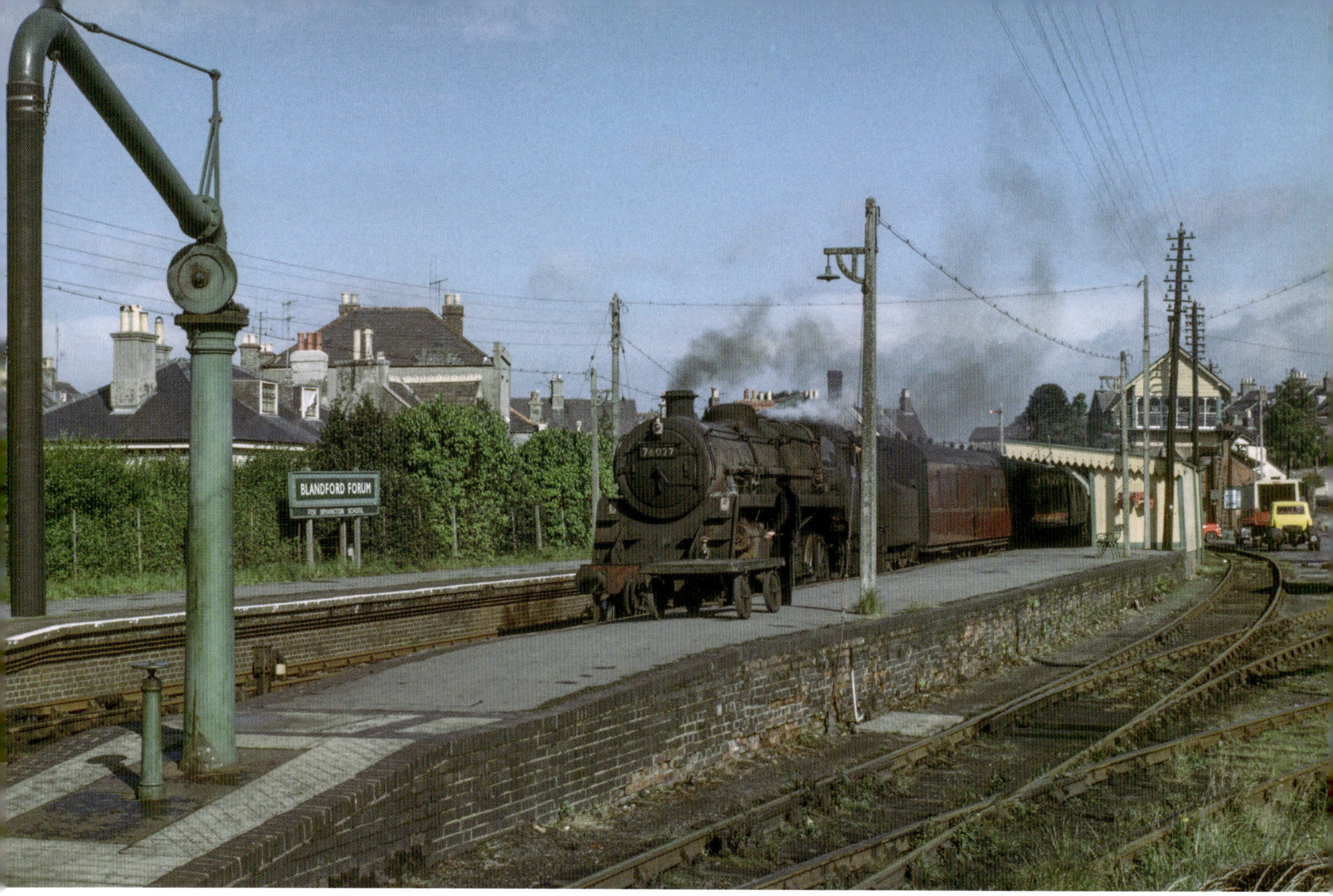
BLANDFORD FORUM
76027

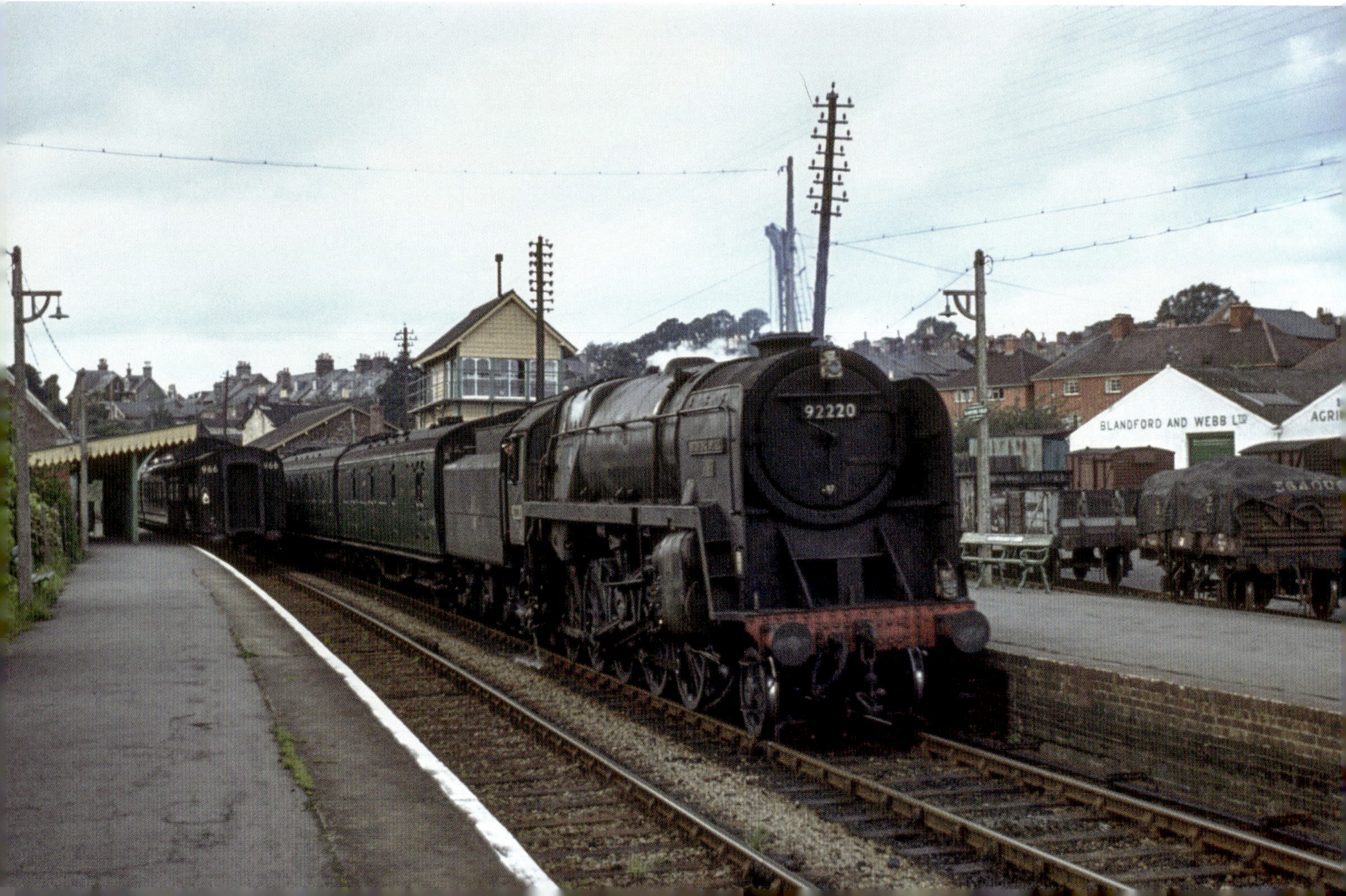
92220
BLANDFORD AND WEBB LTD

# The writing on the wall

Opposite top: No. 76027 is at the head of the 17:55 Bristol - Bournemouth service at Blandford Forum on Saturday 24th. August 1963. The S&D had none of these Standard Class 4 2-6-0s allocated to its own depots with this example being based at Bournemouth. Blandford was one of the larger centres of population located on the route with a population of 3,400 in 1961 and with the station being reasonably conveniently placed for the town centre. *S&DRT*

Opposite bottom: No. 92220 *Evening Star* heads the 15:35 Bristol - Bournemouth at Blandford Forum on Saturday 24th. August 1963. This service was due here at 18:20 and was scheduled to arrive at Bournemouth West at 19:05. If no passengers for the next station, Bailey Gate, had given notice to the guard then the train would not stop there but continue on to Broadstone. At the end of the summer service No. 92220 had been transferred away from the S&D to Cardiff East Dock but surprisingly returned the following year even though its services were no longer required to haul any long distance through trains. In 1963 a request had been made for two Black 5s in July to assist the motive power shortage caused by non availability of so many locomotives at Bath. Harold Morris, the Bath shedmaster was particularly annoyed at having to allocate these large 2-10-0s to such mundane tasks as hauling three and four coach locals. The 9Fs arrived with no steam heating facility, so could not be used after September, additionally they could not be turned on the turntables at Evercreech Junction or Templecombe so freight work was largely outside their scope. These giants therefore spent their days ambling along with three of four coach featherweight loads. As can be imagined this caused much resentment as they were very heavy on coal and provided far too much power for the work required. *S&DRT*

Top: Collett No. 3206 departs from the former Wells branch platform at Glastonbury with a goods service for Evercreech Junction on 8th. September 1962 passing the tall co-acting starting signal, the repetition of signal arms being necessary here due to the restricted view available to drivers of approaching trains caused by the intervening glazed footbridge. The lowest signal arm, marked "S", controlled shunting movements and on the right can be seen a saw mill which had its own private siding. The white post just visible to the right of the locomotive smokebox is part of Dyehouse Lane level crossing which today sports replica gates erected as a memorial to the importance of the railway to the towns of Glastonbury and Street. *Douglas Twiball*

Bottom: The traditional view of the S&D platforms at Highbridge taken from the footbridge on the 8th. September 1962 reveals the extensive layout with platforms 1-4 on the left and the longer platform 5 on the right which handled arrivals and formerly served as the departure platform for services which continued to Burnham-on-Sea. The former Works buildings can be seen in the right background behind the bracket signal with the engine shed to the right of the signal box. An unidentified Collett 0-6-0 waits at platform 2/3 with the next departure for Evercreech Junction and Templecombe. *Douglas Twiball*

## Somerset & Dorset Demise

Above: This is the view from the S&D's platform 5 at Highbridge looking over the flat crossing with the GWR main line to the Burnham-on-Sea line beyond. With platforms numbered 1-7 one might have expected a variety of destinations to be on offer at Highbridge. However, although the notice on the footbridge directs the passenger to platforms 1, 2, 3 & 4 to the right they, following the cessation of passenger services from Burnham, merely handled departing services for Evercreech Junction and Templecombe which could have been comfortably accommodated at one platform. Platform 7 over the bridge to the left was for Bristol whilst access to platform 6 for Exeter did not require the services of the footbridge being to the left of platform 5. No less than three signal boxes are visible in this view being, from left to right, the GWR box "Highbridge Crossing", the S&D box "Highbridge East B" which closed in May 1965 and the former S&D box "Highbridge A" which ceased its function in 1914 when control of the flat crossing was transferred to the GWR box. *Douglas Twiball*

Opposite top: An exotic visitor indeed! What is believed to be the only visit of a Castle class locomotive to Bath Green Park, part of whose train shed roof can just be seen in the background, is captured in this view of No. 7023 *Penrice Castle* carrying reporting No. X05 and sporting an 85A Worcester shedplate. This was prior to working a leg of the Home Counties Railway Society special of 7th. June 1964 which the locomotive would power as far as Gloucester. Notice the gentleman on the right with the loud hailer no doubt to be used to shepherd the railtour participants back to the train whilst the fireman checks to ensure that the headboard is firmly attached. Trespassing over the tracks and alighting from carriages where there was no platform were apparently tolerated in those days before the reign of Health & Safety circumscribed such activities.

Opposite bottom: Last of the S&D 7Fs to remain in service was No. 53807 which made its final trip with the 11:00 goods from Bath to Evercreech Junction on Saturday 5th. September 1964. Although the train was heavily loaded no banker was taken from Radstock for the climb up the Mendips which the 7F took in her stride. As no freight was offering for the return journey the working was cancelled and the trip back was undertaken just "engine and brake". After arriving back at Bath the locomotive was turned, the fire dropped for the last time and the 2-8-0 placed on the withdrawn road at Green Park shed and half a century of service to the line by the class came to an end. In this view it is seen with rusting motion on the withdrawn siding where it remained until December. It was towed away from Bath in mid-December and on Boxing Day was observed on Bristol's Barrow Road shed en route to South Wales for scrapping. By March 1965 it had only made it as far as Severn Tunnel Junction and it was not until April that it finally arrived at Cashmore's yard in Newport. Two of its sister locomotives, Nos. 53808 and 53809, were fortunate enough to have been bought by Woodham's at Barry and both were eventually rescued and returned to steam so that today we can still enjoy the sight and sound of an S&D 7F. *Wilf Stanley*

# 3
# On borrowed time
# (1965 - final full year of operations)

Bath Green Park station was impressive by any standards and our first view reveals Standard Class 3MT No. 82041 awaiting departure from the station with the 11:41 service for Bristol Temple Meads via Mangotsfield on 11th. December 1965. In the winter of 1963/4 for example there were seven departures Mondays-Fridays on this line with an additional service on Saturdays. Come the "Emergency Timetable" of 1966 departures were reduced to just three on Mondays-Fridays, with nothing between 07:15 and 16:00, and four on Saturdays. Had this useful suburban route survived closure it would no doubt have been a godsend today in helping commuters from the east of the city negotiate Bristol's tortuous rush hour traffic. No. 82041 was one of a pair of these useful 2-6-2Ts based at Bath during the 1960s. *Douglas Twiball*

On the 7th. December 1965 Standard Class 4 No. 75072 has just delivered the 11:46 service from Bournemouth into Green Park where it handed over the train to Peak diesel D121 which had taken it on to Bristol Temple Meads. With the road now clear No. 75072 backs out of the terminus in order to make its way to the shed for servicing. *Derek Fear*

# Somerset & Dorset Demise

On borrowed time

Opposite top: Having brought in a previous service and after release from the front of its train, Standard tank No. 82001 passes Peak diesel D17 as it makes its way to shed on 3rd. December 1965. These powerful 1Co-Co1 Sulzer diesels were often used on filling in turns operating workings from Bristol Temple Meads to Green Park before returning to the Midlands and the North with main line services, so the apparent over provision of motive power for these short suburban trains was perhaps not as wasteful as it might have first appeared. D17 entered service in December 1960 and lasted until withdrawal as No. 45024 in October 1980. *Derek Fear*

Opposite bottom: Framed by the magnificent train shed of Bath's Green Park terminus and wreathed in escaping steam, Bournemouth based Standard Class 4 No. 76013 is at the head of the 13:10 to Templecombe on 2nd. December 1965. During its 98 minute journey of 37 miles all thirteen intermediate stations and halts were served. If passengers wished to travel beyond Templecombe there was a connecting service available as far as Blandford Forum but only after enduring a 47 minute wait at Templecombe. Such lax connections as these undoubtedly deterred passengers from travelling and many thought it was all part of a grand plan to run down the line leading to eventual closure. *Derek Fear*

Above: Seen from the end of platform 2 No. 80039 crosses the River Avon bridge to enter Bath Green Park with the 16:18 service from Templecombe on 31st. August 1965. The proximity of this bridge effectively precluded any extension of the rather short platforms at Green Park. Thus, until the end of through services in 1962, stock of the longer trains came to rest on the bridge itself as only nine coaches could be accommodated at the platform requiring passengers in the final few coaches to walk through the train in order to alight. *Derek Fear*

## Somerset & Dorset Demise

Above: On the 9th. October 1965 one of the 45 strong Standard Class 3 2-6-2Ts No. 82001 arrives with the 13:30 service from Bristol Temple Meads consisting of three maroon coaches. This locomotive was based at Bristol Barrow Road shed at this time but would be withdrawn at the end of the year. *Derek Fear*

Opposite top: One of Bath's pair of pannier tank allocated to the depot at this time in September 1965 was No. 3681 seen here in dreadful external condition parked in front of the loading gauge. Pannier tanks had first come to Bath in 1959 following the takeover of the northern half of the line by the WR the previous year. Over the years seven different examples of the 57XX Class were shedded here as were two examples of the 94XX type however, these types always seemed very out of place on the S&D. *Derek Fear*

Opposite bottom; Adjacent to the Bath terminus was the motive power depot where a rear three quarter viewpoint shows off the elegant lines of the Standard 2-6-0 design as represented by No. 76026 seen on 9th. October 1965 waiting to proceed to the shed. *Derek Fear*

# Somerset & Dorset Demise

# On borrowed time

Opposite top: Bournemouth based Standard tank No. 80138 exits the S&D shed roads in a cloud of steam on 11th. September 1965 passing Standard Class 5 No. 73001. The coaling stage can be seen on the right behind the telegraph pole and to the right of that lies the stock of the depot breakdown train in its traditional red livery. *Derek Fear*

Opposite bottom: Seen from the ramp leading to the coaling stage Bournemouth based Standard tank No. 80134 is laying over between trips on the S&D shed on 23rd. September 1965. Being constructed of wood, unlike the stone built Midland shed, with lattice windows and an open wooden girder roof it was something of a miracle that the shed never caught fire during its existence although it did suffer some minor mishaps resulting in the end wall being breached on occasion. Fire was not the only danger for being only slightly above the level of the River Avon flooding was also a hazard experienced here from time to time. It was a four road shed with, at its peak, some 50 locomotives on its allocation. *Derek Fear*

Above: The water softening plant is seen in this view which also includes an ancient sludge tender which carried the wording "To be returned to Water Softening Plant Bath". Standard class 5 No. 73068 completes the picture taken on 11th. September 1965. *Derek Fear*

## Somerset & Dorset Demise

Above: Standard tank No. 80013 is at rest in front of the coaling stage at Green Park depot on 25th. October 1965. A couple of loaded coal trucks can be seen on the incline ready to discharge their loads. This brick built stage was constructed in 1954 replacing the former timber construction. *Derek Fear*

Opposite top: This panorama of 1st. September 1965 shows the approaches to Green Park and reveals several locomotives on view including pannier tank No. 3681 on the right and 8F No. 48760 in the centre of the picture. The stone built Midland shed is visible in the centre background with the wooden S&D shed off to the left where evidence of further locomotives in steam is visible. Hard to believe that this busy scene would be rendered extinct just six months later. On the right is Bath station signalbox which was a 41 lever box to a standard Midland design and which controlled access to the locomotive sheds and Midland Bridge goods yard. This was one of two goods yards at Green Park the other being located to the north of the line near Bath Junction. *Derek Fear*

Opposite bottom: On the 9th. October 1965 a line of condemned locomotives could be seen at Green Park adjacent to the Midland shed. Amongst those on "death row" was Standard Class 5 No. 73054, with sacking over the chimney, which we will see in happier times at Henstridge on page 45. Four days later this 4-6-0 along with classmates 73015 and 73051 would be towed away for scrap being promptly despatched by Cashmore's yard in Newport. *Derek Fear*

# On borrowed time

23

## Somerset & Dorset Demise

Top: Heading on to the S&D proper for a trip down the mainline, Standard tank No. 82030 negotiates the long curve leading from Bath Junction up to Devonshire tunnel which saw the direction of travel change from west to south east with the 13:10 service from Bath Green Park to Templecombe on the 17th. November 1965. The trackbed here now forms part of the footpath and cycle route known as the Bath Linear Park. Although some records show No. 82030 as having been withdrawn from Bristol Barrow Road shed in August 1965 the locomotive appears to have been reinstated and transferred to Green Park from where it was finally withdrawn at the end of the year and placed in store. *Derek Fear*

Bottom: Looking down from Maple Grove pedestrian bridge Standard 2-6-4T No. 80059 approaches Devonshire tunnel on the 1 in 50 climb up Devonshire bank with the 15:20 service from Bath to Templecombe on 21st. October 1965. *Derek Fear*

Opposite: Bathed in afternoon sunlight No. 76026 runs down through Horsecombe Vale towards Midford with the 16:20 Bath - Bournemouth Central service on Saturday 9th October 1965. This train started from Bristol during the summer but in the winter timetable the origin was Bath whence it ran non stop to Shepton Mallet. Passengers for intermediate stations were catered for by the following 16:35 service which called at all stations to Templecombe except Masbury. The southern portal of Combe Down Tunnel can be seen in the background. *S&DRT*

Opposite: An unidentified Standard Class 4 4-6-0 with a 3 coach train in SR green livery, the stripe above a section of the middle coach indicating 1st. Class seating, has just passed the Midford down distant signal before crossing the graceful Tucking Mill viaduct. The superb scenery of much of the route was seldom better than that to be enjoyed in this section between Combe Down tunnel and Midford. The railway seemed to fit naturally into its surroundings only enhancing the scene rather than detracting from it. *Graham Smith courtesy Richard Sissons*

Above: No. 75072 approaches Wellow with the 11:46 from Bournemouth on 13th. October 1965. Piles of sleepers are all that remains of the former goods yard sidings which, following the closure of the goods yard in June 1963, were lifted in June 1964 when the goods yard ground frame was also removed. *Derek Fear*

# Somerset & Dorset Demise

Above: The 09:05 from Templecombe to Bath hauled by Templecombe based Ivatt tank No. 41216 restarts after the Shoscombe & Single Hill halt stop on 3rd. November 1965 and passes over bridge No. 29 known as Single Hill bridge which crossed over a minor road to Frome. After years of campaigning for a halt the residents of Shoscombe finally got their wish in 1929 when MP Sir George Lansbury, who went on to lead the Labour party from 1932-5, opened the halt on 23rd. September. Products of the SR's Exmouth Junction concrete works were used for the platforms, one of which can be seen on the left of this view, following the "harp and slab" construction method. These pre-fabricated components contained integral concrete nameboards and ornate oil lamps. There were no buildings on the platforms but a path to the village had a small booking office and waiting shelter located at the top. Five halts were opened on the S&D in the 1920s but only Shoscombe lasted until the closure of the line indicating how well it was used. *Derek Fear*

Opposite top: Standard 2-6-0 No. 76026 approaches Radstock North with 16:20 service from Bath Green Park to Bournemouth on 11th. October 1965. Following closure of Bournemouth West the previous month most S&D services now terminated at Bournemouth Central. *Derek Fear*

Opposite bottom: With front headcode lamps piercing the gathering gloom Standard tank no. 80041 arrives with 15:20 service from Bath to Templecombe on the afternoon of the 19th. November 1965. Leaving the mainline clear Jinty No. 47276 has retired to the sidings on the right where it is simmering gently awaiting its next turn of duty. *Derek Fear*

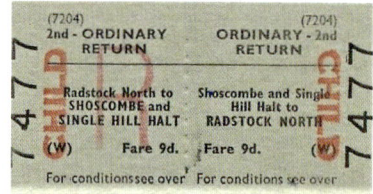

On borrowed time

Somerset & Dorset Demise

Above: This view from the cab of Jinty No. 47276, as it passes milepost 10 ½ returning bunker first to Radstock after a period of shunting at Norton Hill colliery on 23rd. November 1965, affords us a glimpse of Five Arches viaduct in the distance and of the WR Frome – Bristol line on the left. Note the shovel resting on the tank top to avoid cluttering up the rather restricted footplate. *Derek Fear*

Opposite top: No. 80146 coasts downhill to Radstock with the 09:05 Templecombe to Bath service on 6th. August 1965 passing the grass grown spoil heaps of Norton Hill colliery, which was situated just round the corner on the left hand side of the line, apparent behind the coaches. This example of the Standard 4MT tank was Bournemouth based and lasted in service there until the very end of SR steam in July 1967. *Derek Fear*

Opposite bottom: Looking back from the coaches of the 09:48 from Bath Green Park to Bournemouth train on Thursday December 23rd. 1965 as it waits in the platform at Midsomer Norton South station, "Jinty" 0-6-0T No. 47276 can be seen shunting in the sidings at Norton Hill colliery. The underbridge seen behind the coaches crossed Silver Street and the subsequent removal of this structure in November 1969 has rendered any extension of the preservation society's track back to Radstock a particularly expensive undertaking. *Geoff Plumb*

# On borrowed time

## Somerset & Dorset Demise

Above: Seen from the small goods yard at Midsomer Norton No. 73001 leaves with the 09:48 Bath to Bournemouth service on 4th. November 1965. The loading gauge seen in this view has been faithfully recreated by the preservation society based here. Note the metal quadrant board placed behind the up side signal to aid sighting for loco crews. *Derek Fear*

Opposite top: Standard tank No. 80094 which was at the time allocated to Feltham depot is entrusted with the 16:20 Bath to Bournemouth and is seen here heading towards Chilcompton tunnel on 10th. August 1965 through the deep cutting which was subsequently filled with household rubbish after closure. *Derek Fear*

Opposite bottom: Under summer skies Standard Class 5 No. 73001 exits the short Chilcompton tunnel at just 66 yards in length with the 09:48 Bath to Bournemouth service on 14th. July 1965. This locomotive was fitted with a chime whistle which contained two chambers that sounded simultaneously giving that distinctive "American" sound. *Derek Fear*

## Somerset & Dorset Demise

Above: Viewed from bridge No. 52 Baker Robinson's bridge one of Bournemouth shed's stud of Standard 2-6-0s No. 76015 leaves Chilcompton with the 09:05 Templecombe to Bath service on 9th. July 1965. The top of one of the two water towers provided here can be seen above the last carriage. Sheppards sawmill was in the vicinity which accounts for the stacks of timber to be seen to the left of the line. *Derek Fear*

Opposite top: Standard Class 4MT No. 80041 comes charging up the grade into Chilcompton station with the 08:15 from Bath on 23rd. November 1965. A coating of frost lies on the sleepers on this chilly morning. *Derek Fear*

Opposite bottom: Standard Class 5 No. 73001 gets away from the station stop at Chilcompton, unstaffed since February 1964, with 09:48 from Bath Green Park on 27th. November 1965. Further rationalisation at Chilcompton had seen the signalbox closed the previous April and the station sidings and crossover facilities lifted in July 1965. It would appear from the heap of coal on the former goods dock that the yard was still used at this time by the local coal merchant. *Derek Fear*

On borrowed time

# On borrowed time

Opposite top: Standard 2-6-2T No. 82041 passes under Bridge No. 58 Coal Lane bridge on the approach to Moorewood with the 13:10 from Bath on 23rd. November 1965. There were a number of World War II concrete tank traps positioned near to the line in this vicinity and a brick pillbox can be seen on the left of this view. The severe gradients of 1 in 50 and 1 in 55 which had applied all the way from Radstock eased a little here to 1 in 66 with some short stretches of level track which the locomotive crews not doubt appreciated. Climbing continued after Moorewood until the summit at Masbury was reached. *Derek Fear*

Opposite bottom: No. 80037 presents a fine sight as the line passes through frosty fields on the bright winter's morning of 22nd. November 1965 as the train climbs between Chilcompton and Binegar with the 08:15 service from Bath. Cold temperatures were particularly conducive to obtaining shots with plenty of steam condensing. The Mark 1 brake coach (BSK S34615) seen here, although withdrawn from service in 1971, interestingly is still in service with Network Rail as part of their MENTOR (Mobile Electrical Testing, Observation and Recording) set used to ensure that overhead power lines meet the specifications required for the 25kv supply. *Derek Fear*

Above: Passing milepost 14¾ situated between Chilcompton and Binegar No. 73068 is seen with the 09:50 from Bath to Bournemouth on 19th. October 1965. It was quite possible to chase trains by car in this way and to photograph them at several points on the line. This was a reflection of the frequency of stops allied with the gradients preventing high speed running over many sections of the northern half of the route. *Derek Fear*

## Somerset & Dorset Demise

Above: Lonely Masbury Halt situated high up on Mendip witnesses the departure of Standard tank No. 82041 on the 8th. November 1965. Undoubtedly few, if any, passengers had joined or alighted from this service which is the 09:05 from Templecombe to Bath Green Park. Masbury saw just three southbound and this solitary northbound departure daily, a level of service which ironically increased with the introduction of the "Emergency" timetable the following year when four southbound departures were provided. The heap of stones, apparent on the grass bank behind the locomotive cab, was the sad remains of the recently demolished signalbox. *Derek Fear*

Opposite top: No. 73001 has a full head of steam and is raring to go from a wet Shepton Mallet station, though the starting signal is still 'on'. The bridge in the distance carried the GWR branch line from Witham to Wells and Yatton, part of which is still in use to Merehead and another part forms the East Somerset Railway from Cranmore. The Standard Class 5 is at the head of the 09:48 train from Bath Green Park to Bournemouth on 23rd December 1965. *Geoff Plumb*

Opposite bottom: Prior to No. 80059 restarting the 15:20 service from Bath to Templecombe from Shepton Mallet's Charlton Road station on 12th. October 1965 the crew seen on the platform appear to be concerned about something amiss on the locomotive. By this time the condition of much of the motive power then available left a lot to be desired. *Derek Fear*

In the days when mail was an important traffic for the railways this timeless scene depicts the oft repeated ritual of loading and unloading mailbags from the guard's van. The guard, with green flag in hand, has to temper his impatience to signal "right away" whilst the loco crew are busy replenishing their steed from the up platform water crane at Evercreech Junction. *Graham Smith courtesy Richard Sissons*

A northbound service makes its way over bridge No. 95 the eleven arch 121 yard Prestleigh Viaduct slogging up the 1 in 50 grade from Evercreech New to Cannard's Grave prior to its stop at Shepton Mallet. No less than thirteen minutes were allowed in the schedule for passenger trains to traverse the 3¼ miles between these two stations giving an average speed of 15 mph no doubt reflecting the severity of the gradient. Heavy goods trains were often reduced to walking pace when negotiating the viaduct which crossed a tributary of the River Alham. *Douglas Twiball*

On borrowed time

Top: Bruton road level crossing to the south of Evercreech Junction witnesses the passage of Standard 4-6-0 No. 73001 with the 09:48 from Bath to Bournemouth on 10th. December 1965. The appropriately named Fred and Freda Box were the resident crossing keepers here from 1938 until closure of the line in 1966. A small lever frame cabin, the side of which can be seen on the left of this view, was situated adjacent to the keeper's cottage which was of Somerset Central origin. Today merely a gap in the hedge marks the site of this former crossing. *Derek Fear*

Bottom: A foggy winter's day at Wincanton sees No. 73068 exit the staggered platforms passing the goods shed on the right with the 09:48 from Bath to Bournemouth on 19th. November 1965. In the distance on the up line Ivatt tank No. 41223 will shortly be collecting a couple of cattle wagons dropped off by the departing train. *Derek Fear*

# On borrowed time

Opposite: No. 76014 has charge of the 13.20 service to Bristol, which rather inconveniently started from Branksome rather than Bournemouth Central, on Saturday 6th. November 1965. This was no doubt all part of the plan to make the remaining services over the line as unattractive to the travelling public as possible. This view was taken at the attractive Wyke Lane (Bridge No. 116) north of the point where the S&D crossed over the Great Western main line between Cole and Evercreech Junction. The photographer recorded the time of his shot as 15:00 so the service was running pretty well to schedule. *S&DRT*

Top: Templecombe Joint station on a very miserable Thursday 23rd. December 1965, looking towards Exeter. Maroon liveried "Warship" class 42 No. D870 "Zulu" is departing with a train from Waterloo to Exeter consisting of green Bulleid coaches, while on the right in the Somerset & Dorset yard is BR Standard 2-6-4T No. 80037, with Ivatt 2-6-2T No. 41283 just visible way down in the sidings. D870 was built at Swindon Works and entered service in October 1961, the last of the Class 42s, and was allocated to Laira depot, Plymouth, until May 1966, then transferring to Newton Abbot. It remained there until August 1967 when it returned to Laira where it was eventually stored from 14th August 1971 and withdrawn from 28th. August 1971. By January 1972 it was back at Swindon Works with just a derelict shell remaining, the final breaking up taking place by May 1972 after a service life of just under ten years. *Geoff Plumb*

Bottom: No. 73001 has arrived at Templecombe station with the 09:48 train from Bath Green Park to Bournemouth West. It is standing at the island platform which has the L&SWR main line at its opposite face. On departure from here it had to reverse back to the S&D main line and then set forward again to pass under the L&SWR line. On the left is LMS Ivatt 2-6-2T No. 41283 shunting some stock in the S&D side of the yard. The Standard Class 5 was built at Derby Works in May 1951 and on entering service was allocated to Derby and then to Shrewsbury in March 1956 via a short sojourn at Bristol St. Philips Marsh depot. It didn't remain long at Shrewsbury either, moving to Swindon by December 1956. By January 1964 it was back in Bristol, though this time at Barrow Road shed, moving once again to Gloucester Horton Road in January 1965. It was only there for a month or so before its final move to Bath Green Park from March 1965 to work out its final days over the S&D. It was withdrawn a few days after this photograph was taken, on 31st December 1965, and stored at Bath until April 1966, after which it ended up at Cashmore's, Newport, where it was scrapped during May 1966. Templecombe station was closed along with the S&D from March 1966 and the buildings demolished during 1968, though the signal box remained in use. The LSWR main line was largely reduced to single track but eventually, due to local demand and backed by volunteer efforts, the station was re-opened in October 1983 with the signal box becoming the booking office. *Geoff Plumb*

# Somerset & Dorset Demise

Above: Standard tank No. 80039 prepares to draw the 09:48 Bath to Bournemouth service, which had stopped at Templecombe Upper station, back down the spur to Templecombe No. 2 Junction in order that the train may proceed on its way to Bournemouth on 3rd. August 1965. In order to make connections with the SR mainline services and to accommodate the bizarre manoeuvres required at Templecombe, passengers on this service had to endure a wait of no less than 36 minutes here. *Derek Fear*

Opposite top: A dramatically lit panorama of Templecombe shed yard under threatening skies reveals a fine collection of 1960s cars no doubt belonging to shed staff or possibly to visiting enthusiasts and the sad sight of withdrawn locomotives including an Ivatt tank, Standard Class 4 and a Standard tank standing on the former eastern spur line to the LSWR mainline which was closed as early as 1870. Part of the depot's breakdown train comprising an ex LSWR carriage used as a Mess & Tool Van was parked in front of the goods shed and provided a vivid splash of colour. The former stone built Dorset Central station building, subsequently used by the motive power department, can be seen on the far left with the 50 foot turntable located just behind. *Jeremy Staines*

Opposite bottom: The Standard Class 5 4-6-0s were well liked by S&D enginemen ever since the introduction of the first trio to Green Park shed from new in June 1954 but this green liveried example seen here at Henstridge, No. 73054, did not arrive at 82F until April 1961. The driver looks back along the short platform as a handful of passengers leave the train. Although the village was reasonably close to the station and had a population of some 1100 souls passenger business at the station was light and the goods facilities comprised just one siding, controlled by a ground frame, which judging by the rust on the rails had seen no traffic for some time. *Graham Smith courtesy Richard Sissons*

On borrowed time

# Somerset & Dorset Demise

*Opposite top:* Following the temporary closure of Bournemouth West station from 6th. September 1965, which in fact turned out to be permanent, most S&D services were diverted to Bournemouth Central. No. 80041 rests on the depot at Bournemouth after arrival with the 12:30 service from Templecombe on 22nd. September 1965. *Derek Fear*

*Opposite bottom:* Returning to Evercreech Junction for a trip down the former mainline now relegated to branch status, the rural nature of this country junction is epitomised in the stack of hay bales seen in the field behind the sign – the junction really was in the middle of nowhere. Staff at such locations often had ample time to ensure that floral displays, such as the one beneath the running in board, were maintained and Evercreech Junction often won certificates for best kept station. *Graham Smith courtesy Richard Sissons*

*Right:* "Fire devils" were a common sight at water cranes to reduce the risk of the water freezing in inclement weather. This rusting example occupied a position in between the two tracks at Evercreech Junction next to the water crane which primarily served down trains, there being another crane at the end of the up platform. Notice the red post box situated in the wall of the building, a common sight often to be found at railway stations. *Graham Smith courtesy Richard Sissons*

## Somerset & Dorset Demise

On borrowed time

Opposite top: Both driver and fireman on board Ivatt 2MT 2-6-2T No. 41291 seem interested in the cameraman as the locomotive arrives from the sidings to form a branch train to Highbridge from Evercreech Junction on Thursday 23rd. December 1965. The train consists of a bogie GUV, possibly in BR (S) green livery, and a maroon liveried brake second coach. *Geoff Plumb*

Opposite bottom: Ivatt tank No. 41206 runs bunker first into Pylle halt on 12th. October 1965 with the usual payload for this lightly used line namely one coach and a van. Note the row of fire buckets attached to the station building – not that there was anyone around to use them to douse any conflagration as the station had been unstaffed since November 1957. The nameboard carrying the suffix "Halt" added in brackets reflects its lowered status. Since 1929 the former signalbox here acted purely as a ground frame although home and distant signals in each direction were retained. *Derek Fear*

Above: With a characteristic bark the Ivatt makes a noisy and smoky exit from Pylle halt passing underneath bridge No. 243 which carried the A37 Fosseway main road from Shepton Mallet to Yeovil. Pylle station at 225 feet above sea level was nearly at the summit of the branch. *Derek Fear*

## Somerset & Dorset Demise

No. 41291 makes a steamy departure from the stop at West Pennard with the 09:45 from Highbridge to Templecombe on 10th. November 1965. Lifting of the down line here had removed the only crossing point on the branch between Glastonbury and Evercreech Junction. The abandoned Goods Shed is seen on the right and today has been converted into residential accommodation. The A361 road can be seen on the far left leading up the hill to West Pennard village and onwards to Glastonbury. The signalbox which formerly housed a 23 lever frame is seen at the end of the platform and was demolished the following year.

The isolated station at Shapwick sees the arrival of the single coach and van constituting the 13:15 service from Evercreech Junction to Highbridge on 10th. November 1965 in the capable hands of Ivatt tank No. 41216. This was a recent arrival at Templecombe shed having been transferred from Exmouth Junction in June. The stations on the branch suffered from being badly positioned in relation to the settlements they served and Shapwick was no exception being two miles north of the village of the same name and one mile south of Westhay. A couple of sidings were provided here to serve local peat workings. *Derek Fear*

Ivatt tank No. 41307 is propelling the 15:40 milk train from Bason Bridge towards Highbridge on the afternoon of Monday 11th October 1965. Bason Bridge to Highbridge was to be one of the few remaining portions of the S&D to see trains after passenger closure as milk traffic from the creamery continued until October 1972. *S&DRT*

# Somerset & Dorset Demise

Left: This shot of the S&D's platform 2 at Highbridge is noteworthy for the bronze war memorial panel, dedicated to those S&D employees who served in World War 1, seen on the end wall of the building. The panel was unveiled in May 1922 and originally sited in the locomotive works, having been designed by an S&D apprentice and made in the Highbridge workshops. It was unveiled by Sir Alan Garrett Anderson a director of the Midland Railway and of the Somerset and Dorset Joint Committee with a blessing performed by the Bishop of Bath & Wells. The panel was moved again shortly before closure of the S&D to the Garden of Remembrance in Highbridge and was awarded Grade II listed status in 2016. It contains the names of 13 employees who died together with a further 153 who served in the armed forces and survived. The wording records that "This tablet is erected by their fellow workers in memory of the men who left the Loco Carriage and Wagon department of the Somerset and Dorset Joint Railway to serve with the forces during the Great War." *Douglas Twiball*

Bottom: Ivatt tank No. 41290 returns light engine over the S&D flat crossing at Highbridge after having shunted loaded milk tanks, which it had brought in on the 15.40 service from Bason Bridge on Sunday 10th. October 1965, into sidings in the WR area of the station for collection and onward transmission to London. This traffic would have previously been handled via the S&D going eastwards to Templecombe and up to the capital via the LSWR mainline but now it travelled westwards to Highbridge and thence over Western Region lines to London. This rerouting was all part of the Western Region's deliberate policy of transferring freight away from the S&D in a bid to bolster the case for closure. S&DRT

Opposite top: We now put the spotlight on the Jinty 0-6-0Ts which played an important role banking and shunting on the S&D. Sunlight filters through the wooden roof trusses illuminating Jinty 3F No. No. 47506 with a rusting chimney and smokebox door surround inside the two road shed at Radstock on 10th. October 1965. The locomotive was in a condition that was unfortunately very typical of S&D motive power in the dying days of the line. *Derek Fear*

Opposite bottom: Being a railway employee the photographer, Derek Fear, had no trouble in "cabbing" a ride on Jinty No. 47506 from Radstock North station down to the shed on 11th October 1965 and he is seen here on the footplate alongside the driver. Derek had worked as a junior clerk at Midsomer Norton & Welton in the 1950s until he transferred to Radstock West in December 1956 remaining there until passenger closure came in November 1959 when he then moved across to the S&D at Midsomer Norton South. *Derek Fear*

# Somerset & Dorset Demise

# On borrowed time

Opposite top: Jinty No. 47276 takes water from the crane positioned outside Radstock shed on 23rd. November 1965. Waste products resulting from the local coal mining activity can be seen in the form of slag heaps forming the dramatic backdrop to this scene. *Derek Fear*

Oppose bottom: Seen from the station footbridge Jinty No. 47276 reverses back into the sidings at Radstock North on 14th July 1965. Waterloo Road seen on the far left and running parallel to the line provided a good vantage point from which to watch proceedings. *Derek Fear*

Above: This view taken inside the shed at Green Park on 11th. September 1965 shows Jinty No. 47276 which was chosen to feature in the black comedy film "The Wrong Box". Several scenes were filmed in Bath including one in Green Park station where a period atmosphere and a suitably antique looking locomotive were required. Rolling stock was provided by three former Barry Railway coaches and the locomotive was painted green with its first and last numbers blacked out. However, true to form the scene in the station lasted only 35 seconds in the finished film! Based on an 1889 novel by R L Stevenson and directed by Bryan Forbes it featured such acting luminaries as John Mills, Ralph Richardson and Michael Caine, with comedy provided by Peter Sellers, Tony Hancock, Peter Cook and Dudley Moore. *Derek Fear*

# Somerset & Dorset Demise

# On borrowed time

Opposite top: Bath Road open day held on 23rd. October 1965 hosted no less than eight steam locomotives several of which feature in this panorama plus a number of diesels including the blue liveried Bristol Pullman, Paxman hydraulic D9517 and just in shot on the far right can be seen the unmistakeable bulbous nose of a Warship No. D800 "Sir Brian Robertson". For the record the steam locomotives were No. 7029 Clun Castle, Nos. 6141, 3659, 47276, 6859 "Yiewsley Grange", 7924 "Thorneycroft Hall" plus Great Western Society locomotives Nos. 6435 and 1420 which were en route from Worcester to Totnes and the Dart Valley Railway. No. 7435 had piloted No. 7029 on a special from Gloucester the previous Sunday with No. 1420 following on behind. In the far distance are a green liveried Class 47 plus a Warship with a Hymek lurking behind the supports of the water tower. *Derek Fear*

Opposite bottom: Jinty No. 47276 was also on display having travelled over from Bath Green Park and it still wore some of its green paint with which it had been adorned for filming purposes. A crowd of eager lads swarm over the Jinty. This Fowler 0-6-0 would last until the end of services on the S&D in March the following year. The modern diesel depot, also now a thing of the past, is evident in the background. *Derek Fear*

Above: Radstock West Freight. Turning now to the "other railway" at Radstock we see pannier tank No. 3735 engaged in shunting Radstock West yard on 30th. June 1965. This was always quite a busy place for freight even after withdrawal of the passenger service in 1959. *Derek Fear*

## Somerset & Dorset Demise

Above: The last day of steam working on the Frome - Radstock line on 4th. September 1965 is caught on film as pannier tank No. 4636 takes on water. Note the bucket conveniently perched on the rear of the locomotive bunker. Steam operations ceased completely from Westbury shed on this date. *Derek Fear*

Opposite top: In July 1965 this point disc (ground signal) was photographed in Radstock West yard. This was believed to be the last example of its type remaining in the Bristol Division. *Derek Fear*

Opposite bottom: On 17th. July 1965 No. 9790 seeks refreshment from the Radstock West yard water crane whilst the crew pose for the photographer. The wagon on the left was one of the tankers that supplied the bitumen terminal at Mells Road further down the line towards Frome and from its pristine condition looks as if it has recently been refurbished at the Marcroft wagon works out of shot on the left behind the photographer. *Derek Fear*

# On borrowed time

**Opposite top:** Green liveried Hymek D7007 prepares to leave Radstock West yard for Bristol East depot with the afternoon goods service consisting of wooden bodied wagons, box vans and steel mineral wagons on 2nd. September 1965. The substantial brick built Goods Shed dates from 1874 and was the second such shed built to serve Radstock goods yard. It contained one through siding with a loading dock within. *Derek Fear*

**Opposite bottom:** Hymek D7051 enters the former Radstock West station with the afternoon freight for Bristol East depot on 10th. August 1965. Steam age equipment is still in situ in the shape of the water crane at the end of the remaining down platform although by this time steam's days were numbered as the WR had vowed to rid itself of this form of traction by the end of the year. The S&D, always a thorn in the side of the WR, ensured that this did not happen by stubbornly operating steam until closure came in March 1966. The base of the Bristol bound starting signal was relocated to the position seen here in the middle of the former Frome bound platform to improve sighting for crews made necessary by the construction of the row of shops seen on the right on the site of the former Bristol platform. *Derek Fear*

**Above:** Another member of the class, D7046 passes Old Mills colliery sidings to the west of Midsomer Norton with the 11:00 freight service from Radstock to Bristol East depot on 9th. July 1965. The sinking of Old Mills pit took place in 1861 and in spite of modernisation following nationalisation in 1947 the coal washery there closed in 1962 with complete closure of the colliery following on 1st. April 1966. The locomotive shed seen on the left latterly housed a Ruston & Hornsby 7 ½ ton diesel and the track branching off to the left in front of the shed led to the colliery whose slag heap is prominent in the middle distance. *Derek Fear*

## Somerset & Dorset Demise

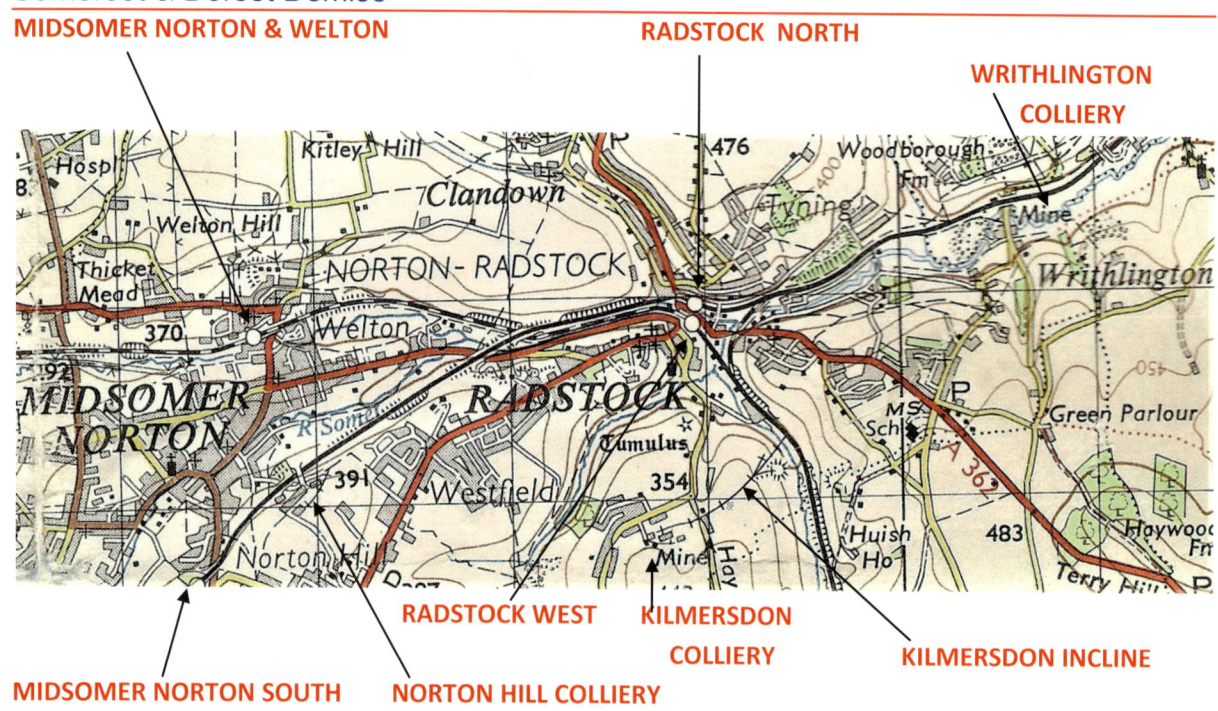

Coal traffic formed a mainstay of S&D freight operations and latterly there were three collieries in the Radstock area.

# On borrowed time

Opposite bottom: This view reveals Norton Hill colliery sidings and pithead wheel visible on the right as Standard Class 5 No. 73051 passes the colliery en route to Midsomer Norton South working hard up the grade with the 09:48 service from Bath to Bournemouth on the 16th. July 1965. No. 73051 spent its whole working life of just over 11 years at Bath. *Derek Fear*

Top: With trucks loaded with the product of Norton Hill mine 8F No. 48525 prepares to leave the colliery sidings for Bath on 16th July 1965. Following withdrawal of the last of the S&D's own 7Fs in 1964 these Stanier machines were the preferred motive power for hauling the heavy coal trains over the route to Bath. This example had arrived at Bath in August 1964 and was one of five of the class working the route at the time of this photograph. The vantage point of the colliery sidings affords a good view of the market town of Midsomer Norton lying spread out in the valley below. *Derek Fear*

Bottom: Against a backdrop of the pithead winding gear at Norton Hill colliery Jinty No. 47276 and 8F No.48706 were captured on 23rd. November 1965. It came as a something of a shock when it was announced that the colliery would close the following February just a few weeks before the S&D itself. Considerable sums of money had been spent in recent years in modernising the pit which made its closure all the more unexpected. The first shaft had been sunk at Norton Hill back in 1839 and the mine eventually became the most productive in the coalfield with 149,000 tons of coal being extracted in 1949. The main line can be glimpsed at a considerably lower level on the left of this view. *Derek Fear*

## Somerset & Dorset Demise

Top: NCB Hunslet No. 1684 is seen at Norton Hill colliery sidings on 4th. November 1965. This 0-4-0T was built in 1931 for Hall & Co. who used it at their Stoat's Nest lime quarry at Coulsdon near Redhill. After several moves it arrived in Somerset from Port Talbot in 1964 to assist the resident Norton Hill Peckett "Lord Salisbury". It was subsequently transferred to nearby Kilmersdon colliery but saw little use there. After withdrawal it was exhibited at the Bleadon & Uphill Railway Museum following which it was purchased by the GWR 1338 Locomotive Fund and is currently awaiting restoration at the Middleton Railway in Leeds where it goes by the name of "Mendip Collier". It was fitted with a Belpaire firebox and outside Walschaerts valve gear, both items being relatively rare features of British industrial locomotive design. *Derek Fear*

Bottom: This view of the 1929 built Peckett 0-6-0ST No. 1788 shunting a loaded coal wagon near the top of Kilmersdon incline leading down to the WR Frome – Radstock line was taken on 16th. November 1966. In spite of output increasing from Kilmersdon colliery in the early part of 1973 the pit here closed in November of that year. This was mainly due to the rapidly dwindling workforce and the difficulty in recruiting miners locally.
*Derek Fear*

Opposite: The incline at Kilmersdon seen on 29th. August 1967. Looking down the 400 foot long incline we can see a loaded coal truck descending on the left and an empty wagon ascending on the right. Constructed in 1877 this cable operated incline had a gradient which varied from 1 in 4.3 at its steepest to 1 in 9.5 at the foot of the incline. A stone building at the top of the incline housed the winding drum and the speed of descent of the wagons was controlled by the loco crew operating a pair of levers in front of the drum house. *David Wigley*

# 4
# Last Gasp (1966)

Opposite top: Having arrived back at the pit head the Peckett will shunt the 16 ton metal mineral wagons to await refilling whilst a coal lorry has backed up to a wooden bodied wagon for coal to be shovelled into sacks and transferred to the road vehicle for local distribution. Truly a labour intensive industrial scene from yesteryear. *Derek Fear*

Opposite bottom: This view of Writhlington colliery shows to advantage the rural nature of its surroundings. Following the end of coal production which came on 28th. September 1973 the final wagonload of coal was not hauled away from the surface stockpiles until some six weeks later on the 16th. November. The line from Radstock to the colliery officially closed three days later. It was hoped at one time that the mine could be preserved to form a mining museum similar to the Big Pit museum which opened subsequently at Blaenavon but sadly these plans came to nothing. *Derek Fear*

Above: On the first day of 1966 Ivatt tank No. 41296 leaves Highbridge with the 14:18 service to Templecombe consisting of a coach and van. In a few days' time, under the provisions of the "Emergency" timetable, just two departures daily were scheduled from Highbridge along the branch rather than the five provided previously. *Derek Fear*

## REVISED SERVICE - WEEKDAYS ONLY
## COMMENCING MONDAY, 3rd JANUARY, 1966

### BOURNEMOUTH TO BATH GREEN PARK

| | | | | | | | SX | SO | | |
|---|---|---|---|---|---|---|---|---|---|---|
| BOURNEMOUTH CENTRAL | dep. | | 06b53 | | 09 37 | — | 15 37 | 15 43 | 17 37 | 18 46 |
| Branksome | | | 07b00 | | 09 44 | 13 25 | 15 44 | 15 50 | 17 43 | 18 53 |
| Parkstone | | | 07 05 | | 09 48 | 13 29 | 15 48 | 15 53 | 17 47 | 18 57 |
| Poole | | | 07b10 | | 09 53 | 13 34 | 15 54 | 16 00 | 17 55 | 19 05 |
| Creekmoor Halt | | | 07b15 | | 09 58 | 13 39 | 16 00 | 16 05 | 18 01 | 19 10 |
| Broadstone | | | 07 32 | | 10 02 | 13 44 | 16 05 | 16 09 | 18 05 | 19 14 |
| Bailey Gate | | | 07 42 | | 10 12 | 13 54 | 16 15 | 16 19 | 18 15 | 19 24 |
| Blandford Forum | | | 07 52 | | 10 25 | 14 05 | 16 26 | 16a30 | 18 27 | 19 34 |
| Shillingstone | | | 08 10 | | 10 36 | 14 15 | 16 42 | | 18 37 | 19 44 |
| Sturminster Newton | | | 08 16 | | 10 42 | 14 21 | 16a49 | | 18 43 | 19 50 |
| Stalbridge | | | 08 23 | | 10 49 | 14 28 | | | 18 50 | 19 57 |
| Henstridge | | | 08 28 | | 10 54 | 14 33 | | | 18 55 | 20 02 |
| TEMPLECOMBE | arr. | | 08 37 | | 11 03 | 14 42 | | | 19 04 | 20 11 |
| | dep. | 07 00 | 08 20 | | | 14 00 | 15 30 | 16 18 | | 20 20 |
| Wincanton | | 07 07 | 08 28 | | | 14 08 | 15 38 | 16 26 | | 20 27 |
| Cole | | 07 16 | 08 39 | | | 14 17 | 15 47 | 16 34 | | 20 37 |
| Evercreech Junction | arr. | 07 23 | 08 44 | | | 14 23 | 15 53 | 16 39 | | 20 43 |

| | | | | | | | |
|---|---|---|---|---|---|---|---|
| Evercreech Junction | dep. | | | 08 45 | | | 17 15 |
| Pylle Halt | | | | V | | | 17 19 |
| West Pennard | | | | 08 55 | | | 17 27 |
| Glastonbury & Street | | | | 09 06 | | | 17 38 |
| Ashcott | | | | 09 12 | | | 17 46 |
| Shapwick Halt | | | | 09 17 | | | 17 51 |
| Edington Burtle | | | | 09 22 | | | 17 57 |
| Bason Bridge | | | | 09 28 | | | 18 05 |
| Highbridge for Burnham-on-Sea | arr. | | | 09 33 | | | 18 10 |

| | | | | | | | |
|---|---|---|---|---|---|---|---|
| Evercreech Junction | dep. | 07 25 | | 14 25 | | 16 40 | 20 45 |
| Evercreech New | | 07 31 | | 14 31 | | 16 46 | 20 51 |
| Shepton Mallet Charlton Road | | 07 52 | | 14 44 | | 16 59 | 21 00 |
| Masbury Halt | | — | | | 17 09 | | |
| Binegar | | 08 08 | | 14 58 | 17 15 | | V |
| Chilcompton | | 08 14 | | 15 04 | 17 21 | | |
| Midsomer Norton South | | 08 19 | | 15 09 | 17 26 | | 21 22 |
| Radstock North | | 08 24 | | 15 14 | 17 31 | | 21 27 |
| Shoscombe & Single Hill Halt | | 08 30 | | 15 20 | 17 37 | | 21 33 |
| Wellow Halt | | 08 34 | | 15 24 | 17 41 | | V |
| Midford Halt | | 08 40 | | 15 30 | 17 47 | | V |
| BATH GREEN PARK | | 08 50 | | 15 40 | 17 57 | | 21 50 |

b — On Saturdays Bournemouth Central dep. 07 05, Branksome 07 12, Poole 07 19, Creekmoor Halt 07 24.   f — NOT Saturdays
V — Calls to set down passengers on notice being given to the guard

---

**BRITISH RAILWAYS**
**WESTERN AND SOUTHERN REGIONS**

**SOMERSET AND DORSET LINE**

**REVISION OF PASSENGER TRAIN SERVICES FROM**

**3rd JANUARY 1966**

UNTIL FURTHER NOTICE

---

This page: The restricted service from 3rd. January 1966.

Opposite top: The LCGB "Mendip Merchantman" railtour of 1st. January 1966 rolls into Highbridge with a brace of Ivatt tanks at the head. No. 41307 leading No. 41283 had left Templecombe fourteen minutes late but this had been reduced to a ten minute deficit by the time the tour arrived at Highbridge. This tour was scheduled for this date as it was expected that the line would close at this time. *Mark Warburton courtesy Mrs M Warburton*

---

## REVISED SERVICE - WEEKDAYS ONLY
## COMMENCING MONDAY, 3rd JANUARY, 1966

### BATH GREEN PARK TO BOURNEMOUTH

| | | | | | | | | SX | SO |
|---|---|---|---|---|---|---|---|---|---|
| BATH GREEN PARK | dep. | | 06 45 | 08 15 | | 16 25 | 18 10 | | |
| Midford Halt | | | 06 57 | 08 27 | | 16 37 | 18 22 | | |
| Wellow Halt | | | 07 03 | 08 34 | | 16 44 | 18 29 | | |
| Shoscombe & Single Hill Halt | | | 07 07 | 08 38 | | 16 48 | 18 33 | | |
| Radstock North | | | 07 13 | 08 44 | | 16 54 | 18 39 | | |
| Midsomer Norton South | | | 07 20 | 08 51 | | 17 01 | 18 47 | | |
| Chilcompton | | | 07 26 | 08 59 | | 17 09 | 18 55 | | |
| Binegar | | | 07 36 | 09 07 | | 17 17 | 19 03 | | |
| Masbury Halt | | | 07 40 | 09 11 | | 17 21 | 19 07 | | |
| Shepton Mallet Charlton Road | | | 07 50 | 09 18 | | 17 29 | 19 15 | | |
| Evercreech New | | | 07 56 | 09 25 | | 17 35 | 19 21 | | |
| Evercreech Junction | arr. | | 08 00 | 09 29 | | 17 38 | 19 24 | | |

| | | | | | | | | |
|---|---|---|---|---|---|---|---|---|
| Highbridge for Burnham-on-Sea | dep. | 06 55 | | | | 16 00 | | | |
| Bason Bridge | | 06 59 | | | | 16 05 | | | |
| Edington Burtle | | 07 05 | | | | 16 12 | | | |
| Shapwick Halt | | 07 10 | | | | 16 18 | | | |
| Ashcott | | 07 17 | | | | 16 21 | | | |
| Glastonbury & Street | | 07 22 | | | | 16 30 | | | |
| West Pennard | | 07 31 | | | | 16 42 | | | |
| Pylle Halt | | 07 40 | | | | 16 52 | | | |
| Evercreech Junction | arr. | 07 45 | | | | 17 00 | | | |

| | | | | | | | | | |
|---|---|---|---|---|---|---|---|---|---|
| Evercreech Junction | dep. | 07 46 | 08 04 | 09 32 | 16 13 | 17 43 | 19 28 | | |
| Cole | | — | 08 13 | 09 38 | 16 20 | 17 49 | 19 34 | | |
| Wincanton | | 07 53 | 08 22 | 09 47 | 16 29 | 17 57 | 19 43 | | |
| TEMPLECOMBE | arr. | 08 05 | 08 29 | 09 53 | 16 36 | 18 05 | 19 50 | | |
| | dep. | 07 35 | | 09 05 | 12 30 | 16 42 | | | 21 03 | 21 03 |
| Henstridge | | 07 44 | | 09 14 | 12 39 | 16 51 | | | 21 11 | 21 11 |
| Stalbridge | | 07 51 | | 09 19 | 12 47 | 16 55 | | | 21 16 | 21 16 |
| Sturminster Newton | | 07 59 | | 09 27 | 12 54 | 17 06 | | | 21 23 | 21 23 |
| Shillingstone | | 08 06 | | 09 37 | 13 00 | 17 12 | | | 21 29 | 21 29 |
| Blandford Forum | | 08 17 | | 09 47 | 13 10 | 17 22 | | | 21 39 | 21 39 |
| Bailey Gate | | 08 28 | | 09 59 | 13 21 | 17 33 | | 18 32 | | 21 50 |
| Broadstone | | 08 40 | | 10 20 | 13 32 | 17 50 | | 18 44 | 21 58 | 22 04 |
| Creekmoor Halt | | 08 44 | | 10 26 | 13 36 | 17 54 | | — | 22 02 | — |
| Poole | | 08 49 | | 10 31 | 13 42 | 18 02 | | 18 57 | 22 13 | 22 13 |
| Parkstone | | 08 56 | | 10 38 | 13 47 | | | | | |
| Branksome | | 09 01 | | 10 42 | 13 51 | 18 10 | | 19 05 | — | — |
| BOURNEMOUTH CENTRAL | | 09 06 | | | 13 57 | 18 15 | | 19 11 | 22 25 | 22 25 |

Bottom: The photographer availed himself of this photographic viewpoint from the footbridge to capture the two tank locomotives about to set back prior to crossing the main WR line via the unusual flat crossing which the S&D made with the GWR on its original route to Highbridge Wharf and Burnham-on-sea. The sunny arrival at Highbridge seen in the previous shot had by this time turned rather wet judging by the puddles on the platform but the showers had done little to dampen the spirits of the passengers thus far although worse was to come. *Derek Fear*

## Somerset & Dorset Demise

# Last gasp

Opposite top: With headboards still attached the train makes its way gingerly over the flat crossing prior to positioning the coaching stock in the down platform at Highbridge (WR). Mass trespass of the tour participants seems to be the order of the day back in 1966 when Health & Safety rules were a lot less rigid. *Derek Fear*

Opposite bottom: Despatched from Bristol Barrow Road shed to Green Park specially to work the railtour onwards from Highbridge to Bath via Bristol 9F No 92243 in appalling external and mechanical condition was declared unfit to proceed with a collapsed brick arch by the time the train had reached Warmley necessitating rescue by 8F No. 48760 leading to an arrival at Bath some hour and a half behind schedule. *Derek Fear*

Top: No. 92243 was one of the last trio of 9F's allocated to Bristol's Barrow Road shed along with Nos. 92209 and 92235. Although some records show it as having been withdrawn from Barrow Road upon closure of that depot on 20th. November 1965, it would appear that it was in fact briefly reallocated to Bath Green Park Shed. The 2-10-0 arrived at Bath in mid-December and was utilised on a Westerleigh freight turn as a trial run. Barrow Road was the last operative steam shed in Bristol and the local newspaper, the Bristol Evening Post, ran an article on the 15th November under the title "Bristol's proud steam age fades out". Unfortunately No. 92243 itself "faded out" by disgracing itself on the special. The grimy 9F is seen here inside the S&D shed on New Year's Day 1966. *Derek Fear*

Bottom: The Bristol depot whence the 9F came is illustrated in this quartet of views taken at Bristol Barrow Road the previous year on 30th. July 1965 when the depot only had a few weeks of life left before closure. In the foreground of this view Modified Hall No. 6965 "Thirlestaine Hall" simmers on shed whilst Standard Class 3 82004 blows off noisily and heads north under clear signals as an unidentified 9F passes by with a southbound goods working. Barrow Road had transferred from the Midland Region to the Western Region back in February 1958. *Derek Fear*

## Somerset & Dorset Demise

Above: With the arches of Barrow Road in the background a grimy Black 5 No. 44764 is seen adjacent to a rather decrepit looking crane that would appear to have seen little use in recent times. An air of dereliction hangs about the place as time was rapidly running out for Bristol's last steam depot. No. 44764 was a long way from home being allocated to Mold Junction at this time. It would be withdrawn in September 1965. *Derek Fear*

Opposite top: Black 5 No. 44805 has its set of front driving wheels dropped for attention at the rear of Barrow Road shed. This was an Oxley based locomotive at this time and following subsequent allocations to Chester, Stoke and Crewe South would remain in traffic until September 1967. *Derek Fear*

Opposite bottom: Condemned locomotives occupy some of the extensive set of sidings in this scene which is dominated by the looming presence of the enormous gasholders in Day's Road. Erected in the 1860s by the Bristol Gas Co. they were demolished in April 1981. By the end of March 1966 withdrawn S&D locomotives from both Green Park and Templecombe sheds would be temporarily stored at Barrow Road awaiting their final journeys to various South Wales scrapyards their number including eight Ivatt tanks, three Standard 4MTs, two Jinties and three 8Fs. *Derek Fear*

# Last gasp

Opposite: The RCTS "Somerset & Dorset" railtour of 2nd. January 1966 was hauled by Maunsell U Class No. 31630 and West Country No. 34015 "Exmouth" These moguls were quite a rarity on the line although examples of the class and of the three cylinder variant U1 had been tried unsuccessfully for a couple of weeks back in March 1954. The trials involved Nos. 31621 and 31906 which operated the 11:40 up service from Bournemouth returning with the 16:25 down service from Bath. This RCTS tour was limited to ten coaches and these two locomotives had taken over from Merchant Navy No. 35011 "General Steam Navigation", which had brought the tour from Waterloo, at Broadstone for the run up to Bath. After arrival there the two locomotives were turned and watered on Green Park shed ready to return light engine to Bournemouth, the tour being taken forward from Bath by 8F No. 48309 to Highbridge. Here a brace of Ivatt tanks would return the tour to Templecombe where No. 35011 was waiting to take the train back to Waterloo. *Derek Fear*

Above: 8F No. 48309 makes a stirring sight with a volcanic exhaust as it leaves Bath Green Park at just after 14:00 for Bristol and Highbridge with the RCTS special of 2nd. January 1966. At Highbridge it would handover to a pair of Ivatt tanks Nos. 41307 and 41283 for a run down the Highbridge branch to Templecombe. *Derek Fear*

## Somerset & Dorset Demise

Top: A lone gas lamp illuminates the truly appalling condition of 57XX Class pannier tank No. 3681 which occupies one of the roads in the Midland shed at Green Park on 1st. January 1966. Amazingly this 0-6-0 would continue in service for a further nine weeks until the last weekend when it was involved in shunting stock for the specials that marked the closure of the line. It even managed to last until 11th. March when it was steamed for the final time in order to haul fellow pannier No. 3758 to Bristol Bath Road depot in the hope that the two tanks might be used on the Clevedon branch which was then the subject of what subsequently proved to be a fruitless preservation attempt. *Derek Fear*

Bottom: Parked out of use on 6th. January 1966 at the side of the stone built Midland locomotive shed Standard Class 5 No. 73001 carries the forlorn chalked inscription "Steam Forever". However, it will not turn a wheel again having been formally withdrawn at the end of 1965 although it had worked once more on the 1st. January 1966 when it was pressed into service to haul the 09:50 Bath to Bournemouth and return working although it was reported as sounding very "off". No. 73001 along with No. 73068 were the last two members of this useful class to be based at Green Park thus ending an association with the S&D stretching back to the arrival of the first examples on the line in June 1954. *Derek Fear*

Opposite: A view of the roadside notice board advertising the presence of Bailey Gate station with the station building and creamery beyond. The informative notice board would not be required for much longer as this was Saturday 5th. March 1966 - the final day of timetabled services on the S&D. The creamery would continue to send milk products away by rail until closure of the remaining freight stub from Broadstone to Blandford Forum in January 1969. *S&DRT*

# Somerset & Dorset Demise

# Last gasp

Opposite top: No. 48706 pauses for water at Evercreech Junction on the southbound GWS special of 5th. March 1966 which terminated at Bournemouth's Central station rather than the S&D's traditional terminus of West station which had closed the previous year. The results of the enthusiasts' efforts, are readily apparent with the white rings on the buffers being particularly noticeable. *Derek Fear*

Opposite bottom: No. 48706 poses on shed at Bournemouth Central prior to being turned and watered for the return trip. The "wasp" stripes of a Drewry diesel shunter can be seen on the right whilst in the left background the unmistakable front end of a Bulleid pacific is evident inside the shed. *Derek Fear*

Above: Parked out of use on 5th. March 1966 this row of condemned locomotives was headed by Standard tank No. 80039 with 8F No. 48444 seen behind. The old carriage body on the left would see no further use for Enginemens' Mutual Improvement classes which had traditionally been held here in years gone by. *Derek Fear*

# Last gasp

Opposite top: Against a clear blue sky No. 41249 obviously has steam to spare judging by the lifting of its safety valves whilst halted at Glastonbury & Street. The inclusion of a Restaurant Car in this LCGB special was something to savour whilst travelling along this bucolic branchline which normally saw only one or two coach local trains. *George Woods*

Opposite bottom: Nos. 34006 "Bude" and 34057 "Biggin Hill" are captured at Chilcompton on the northbound leg during one of the additional photographic stops made on the LCGB tour. The other opportunities for photography had been provided at Glastonbury and at Shepton Mallet, on the southbound leg, all of which caused the special to run late being some 30 minutes behind time upon arrival at Bournemouth Central. Although the gradient eased to 1 in 300 through Chilcompton station the change to a 1 in 50 downgrade to Radstock is very apparent in this view. The special halted here for some ten minutes enabling tour participants seen on the right to obtain their shots. *Mark Warburton courtesy Mrs M Warburton*

Above: Three railway staff are seemingly having a hard time of it turning No. 34057 on the turntable at Green Park after arrival with the LCGB special. "Biggin Hill" would continue in service on the SR until withdrawal from Salisbury shed came in May the following year. In the right background is Standard tank No. 80043 which had arrived earlier with the 07:00 service from Templecombe and would, later that day, take out the 16:25 to Templecombe returning to Bath double heading with No. 80041 at the head of six coaches forming the final northbound working. *George Woods*

# Last gasp

Opposite: A view looking north west at Sturminster Newton, again on the final Saturday of timetabled services, reveals the staggered nature of the two platforms here. Only special railtours ran on the following day. *S&DRT*

Above: Shortly before setting out from Bath the two locomotives of the SLS special of Sunday 6th. March were captured on the bridge over the River Avon, the length of the ten coach train necessitating their positioning here well beyond the end of the rather short platform. The 8F had been in operation the previous day hauling the GWS special for which it had been spruced up by members of the society. *Derek Fear*

Bottom: The SLS Special, commemorating the Somerset & Dorset's passing, gets away southwards from Blandford Forum with 8F 2-8-0 48706 and 4MT 2-6-4T 80043 double-heading, having just passed the northbound RCTS "Somerset & Dorset Farewell" railtour powered by No. 35028 "Clan Line" heading in the opposite direction. *Geoff Plumb*

Above: Nos. 41249 and 41283 pose at Templecombe shed awaiting the RCTS railtour on the S&D's final day, Sunday 6th. March 1966. They would assume command of the tour at Templecombe No. 2 Junction, the special not running up to the main station at Templecombe. Visitors would then be treated to the unusual sight of a Merchant Navy, No. 35028, on Templecombe shed. The buffers of both locomotives had been specially "whitened" for this sad occasion. These were the only two operational locomotives remaining on shed as the other occupants of the depot, Standard 4-6-0s No. 75072 and 75073 were dead in the yard awaiting a tow by No. 34057 to Blandford later that evening. With this movement "Biggin Hill" was to become the last steam locomotive to run on the S&D before official closure at midnight. From Blandford the two Standards would be taken on subsequently to Ringwood for scrapping. *S&DRT*

# Last gasp

*Opposite bottom:* The RCTS headboard has already been removed from the leading locomotive, Ivatt tank No. 41283, but the commemorative wreath is still in place on the smokebox door. The two locomotives then took the tour train across the GWR mainline into the up goods line passing through the Goods Shed and then reversed into the down platform at the WR station where West Country No. 34013 "Okehampton" took over for the run to Mangotsfield. *Geoff Plumb*

*Above:* Bulleid pacific No. 34013 "Okehampton" has vacated the down goods loop where it was waiting for the arrival of the tour and backed onto the tour stock moved from Highbridge S&DJR station to the down platform at the WR station by the two Ivatt tanks that had brought it from Evercreech Junction a short while earlier. It is now ready to depart for Mangotsfield with the RCTS "Somerset & Dorset Farewell" railtour shortly crossing to the up line. *Geoff Plumb*

# 5
# Aftermath (1966 - 1980)

# Aftermath

*Opposite top:* At the Bath Road depot open day on 30th. April 1966 a number of ex Green Park locomotives were on show including Standard tank No.80043 which had been operative on the last day of normal service on the S&D on 5th. March and again the following day on the SLS special when it shared haulage duties with No. 48706. Bath Road depot ceased operations in September 1995 and was demolished in 2003/4. *Derek Fear*

*Opposite bottom:* With its Great Western Society headboard back in place temporarily, which it had carried on the special of 5th. March 1966, Class 8F No. 48706 is seen exhibited at the Bath Road open day of 30th. April 1966 where for the sum of 3/- (15p) one could have one's photograph taken, postcard size and sent to your home address, with what was dubbed rather inaccurately "the last working steam loco" given that steam on BR would continue until August 1968. *Derek Fear*

*Above:* Pylle Hill goods yard near Bristol Temple Meads is well stocked with wagons but of more interest in this view is the quintet of former S&D motive power photographed on the 30th. April 1966. From left to right they were Jinty No. 47506, Standard tanks Nos. 80041 and 80037, Jinty No. 47276 and 8F No.48309. *Derek Fear*

Top: On 6th. May 1966 the combined afternoon freight from Bristol East Depot to Radstock West and North yards arrives at the junction where the newly laid connection to the former S&D line had been opened a couple of months previously. A member of the railway staff stands by to operate the point lever to allow access to the spur. The Hymeks heading the train on this occasion were D7053 leading and D7025. Very little traffic is apparent on the parallel A362 road with just a solitary red car evident on what is today a very busy route linking Radstock with neighbouring Midsomer Norton. *Derek Fear*

Bottom: On 18th. September 1966, some six months after closure, a special train was operated from Radstock to Evercreech Junction to collect fittings and scrap and to allow demolition contractors to view the task awaiting them hauled by Hymek D7039. On arrival at Evercreech Junction the contractors detrained to inspect the railway infrastructure here and no doubt assess the work involved in track removal and demolition. The contract for the stretch of the line northwards from Blandford Forum to Radstock was subsequently let to W.R.Arnott, Young & Co of Bilston Staffordshire with work beginning in the first week of February 1967 from a point one mile north of Blandford. The weed strewn nature of the track here testifies to the lack of use over the past six months. *Derek Fear*

Aftermath

Top: The return journey was made with the Hymek propelling the train from the rear as witness the loco crew seen here in the rear cab. The train is seen halted at Chilcompton with the wagon revealing that a grindstone, wheelbarrow and cement troughing for signalling had been collected en route. *Derek Fear*

Bottom: About to cross over the Radstock North level crossing the contractors' special returns to its starting point with wagons loaded with a variety of recovered items – one wonders how many of these were actually re-used. The trackbed of the former tramway which ran to Middle Pit Colliery is evident in the left foreground. This site also marked the former basin of the Somerset Coal Canal. *Derek Fear*

# Somerset & Dorset Demise

# Aftermath

Opposite top: The LCGB "Dorset & Hants" railtour of 16th. October 1966 attracts a goodly crowd of sightseers and photographers as it rumbles across the level crossing adjacent to Ringwood station with Standards Nos. 77014 and 76026 in control. The locomotives had assumed charge of the train at Broadstone whence they returned after visiting Ringwood on the "Old Road" between Brockenhurst and Poole. The tour would later go on to Blandford and I can vividly recall seeing it flash over the level crossing at Bailey Gate in fine style topped and tailed by the two Standards. *Derek Fear*

Opposite bottom: In order to return to Broadstone, and then make a foray up the S&D to Blandford Forum, the Standard Class 3 assumed its position at the front of the train whilst the Class 4 No. 76026 took up its place at the rear. Ringwood station was still substantially intact at this time passenger services having been withdrawn in May 1964. (There was a further tour to visit Blandford the following year. The Manchester Rail Travel Society (MRTS) special was on 25th. March 1967 with Ivatt tank No. 41320 in charge of its five coach train. After Blandford, the special then proceeded to traverse the Swanage branch before returning the train to Bournemouth Central where West Country No. 34004 "Yeovil" took over for the run back to Southampton.) *Derek Fear*

Above: Attracting the attention of a black cow in the adjacent field NBL, later Type 22, diesel No.D6330 is captured travelling south, with a brace of guards vans in tow, approaching Masbury summit on 17th. May 1967. Unfortunately NBL went bankrupt in 1962 and by the late 1960s withdrawn examples of these locomotives were being used to provide spares to keep remaining class members operating. Type 22s had initially been used on S&D demolition trains but due to their poor reliability they were later superseded by Hymeks. Speeds were limited to just 15 mph as the track was no longer being maintained. *Derek Fear*

## Somerset & Dorset Demise

# Aftermath

**Opposite top:** On the 6th. April 1968 the RCTS operated a DMU on the "Thames & Avon" railtour originating at Paddington and calling in at Swindon Works en route to Radstock. It is seen here halted at the foot of the Kilmersdon colliery incline to allow tour participants to view this piece of industrial archaeology. No steps seem to have been provided so no doubt only the more able bodied passengers were able to negotiate the drop from carriage to ballast! The tour then proceeded to Writhlington colliery and thence to Bristol via the North Somerset line, the last passenger train to traverse this section before it was closed in July of that year. The tour also visited the Portishead branch before returning to London via Badminton. The DMU set 420 comprised cars Nos.51367/59513/59543/51409. *Derek Fear*

**Opposite bottom:** The DMU was then captured as it passed the derelict Radstock South signalbox en route to Radstock West and thence by way of the spur to Radstock North and on to Writhlington colliery. The south box, a Type 2 box with a 21 lever frame which was installed in 1911, had closed in August 1966. *Derek Fear*

**Above:** Viewed from a guards van a recovery train approaches Midsomer Norton South on the former up line hauled by Hymek D7028 on 21st. April 1968. At this date the railhead was situated just south of Masbury with a Class O8 diesel shunter bringing recovered materials back to Binegar whence the Hymek collected them. A lone photographer is occupying the site of the former Norton Hill colliery sidings which were on the level thus indicating the gradient on the mainline at this point. A group of children occupying the former down line by the board crossing were no doubt alerted to the proximity of the train by repeated diesel horn warning blasts. *Derek Fear*

## Somerset & Dorset Demise

Above: Having crossed to the down line at Midsomer Norton station the recovery train continued climbing and is here about to enter Chilcompton tunnel. The use of Hymeks on these trains was to cease a couple of months later in early June 1968 when the demolition contractors' base had reached Midsomer Norton. From then on all trains would be hauled the short distance down to Radstock by Class 08 shunters. *Derek Fear*

Opposite top: On Sunday 16th. June 1968 a rake of fourteen wagons loaded with recovered sleepers ran away from just north of Chilcompton gathering speed on the descent to Radstock. As the points leading into Norton Hill colliery yard were routinely set to provide a trap for such runaways the wagons did not descend to Radstock. Track had already been removed from the colliery sidings so the wagons piled up relatively harmlessly in the yard. Police had been alerted to the runaways by an ex railwayman in Chilcompton village and protected the level crossing in Radstock before the wagons could wreak havoc by colliding with the gates. It is believed that children were responsible for releasing the brakes on the wagons. *Derek Fear*

Opposite bottom: A breakdown train hauled by Hymek D7031 was summoned from Bristol Bath Road depot to assist in the recovery of the wagons. It is seen here on 17th. June traversing the spur between the North Somerset and S&D lines. *Derek Fear*

# Aftermath

## Somerset & Dorset Demise

Top: Paused in the station at Radstock North this shot allows us a view of a steam locomotive tender and crane which formed part of the breakdown train. Note the tender is stocked with coal to feed the steam crane. It is believed that the Bath Road breakdown crane at this time was a Ransome & Rapier 45 ton model. *Derek Fear*

Bottom: Displaying headcode 1Z13, green liveried Brush type 4 No, D1986 prepares to leave Blandford Forum with the final passenger service to visit the station, the LCGB "Hampshireman" special of 3rd. November 1968. A few weeks later Blandford lost its remaining freight service and thus 105 years after the opening of the station in September 1863 it ceased to be a railway served town. D1986 introduced to traffic in January 1966 was scrapped in November 1999. At the other end of the train was electro diesel E6108.

# Aftermath

Top: Illustrating the new order of motive power on the remaining demolition trains is Class 08 shunter D3522 seen halted on the bank from Midsomer Norton by the signal post on 5th. March 1969 in order to collect some trackside materials which can be seen being loaded into one of the wagons. It will be noted that just a single line was in situ at this stage and that the former Norton Hill colliery sidings had already been lifted. *Derek Fear*

Right: On 17th. May 1969 the GWS "Somerset Rambler" tour is about to leave Highbridge S&D platform 5 to take a trip up the remaining freight only stub to Bason Bridge. The abandoned former Works buildings can be seen behind the station sign. *Derek Fear*

# Somerset & Dorset Demise

# Aftermath

Opposite top: Two examples of the unique S&D 7Fs were ultimately preserved fortunately having been sent to Barry scrapyard. No. 53809 spent over 11 years at the yard where it was photographed in June 1966. Note the tablet catching apparatus still attached to the tender. The 2-8-0 had arrived in the yard in August 1964 and was destined to be the 78th. locomotive to leave, in December 1975, for a life in preservation. It is currently based on the North Norfolk Railway on long term loan. *Derek Fear*

Opposite bottom: The other 7F to survive was No. 53808 seen on display, carrying a Pines Express headboard, next to Class AL4 (later Class 84) electric locomotive E3044 which was travelling the country at this time as part of a BR exhibition, at an open day held at Bath Road depot on 17th. October 1970. The 2-8-0 was purchased for £2,500 by the S&D Circle comprising a £750 deposit and monthly terms agreed with Dai Woodham, an unusual arrangement at this time as the scrapyard would normally insist on full payment up front before a locomotive left the yard. The 7F was en route to its new home at Radstock where it arrived on 22nd. October. The locomotive is currently housed on the Mid Hants Railway after a long sojourn on the West Somerset Railway. *Derek Fear*

Above: The GWS/Wirral Railway Club railtour of 14th. November 1970 heads through a very damp Radstock North returning from a visit to Writhlington colliery. The underbridge in the foreground allowed pedestrians and the smallest of cars to avoid the notorious queues at Radstock's level crossing gates. *Derek Fear*

# Aftermath

Opposite top: Bath Midland Bridge plays host to a 3 car cross country DMU set on the special run jointly by the GWS/WRC on 14th. November 1970 under the title "Somerset Rambler II". The tour had earlier visited Radstock, Writhlington colliery, Avonside Wharf in Bristol and would go on to Highbridge for a trip to Bason Bridge. *Derek Fear*

Opposite bottom: During the S&D Circle's open day at Radstock on 29th. August 1971 "Cranford No.2", an 0-6-0ST constructed by W G Bagnall in 1942 one of a batch of six similar locomotives, was in operation offering brake van rides. It had been specifically designed for ironstone quarrying duties in Oxfordshire and Northamptonshire resulting from wartime pressure to expand production. The design catered for the sharp corners often associated with quarry working which would normally limit the operation of six coupled locomotives. The locomotive is currently based at the "Rocks by Rail" ironstone museum at Cottesmore in Rutland. This view, taken from the down platform at Radstock North, reveals the absence of one of the gates at the level crossing. Some timber has been placed across both tracks to mark the limits of access for the preservation society. Initially the operation of brake van rides was restricted to the remaining section of the former up line; it would not be until the following year that running the 1½ miles to Writhlington was sanctioned. The former Market Hall seen on the right now houses Radstock Museum which features a display covering "Somerset Coalfield Life". *Derek Fear*

Above: Class 08 shunter D3169 prepares to move one of the last loads of coal from Writhlington colliery in November 1973. Relatively modern coal hoppers were in use at this time having taken over from the traditional 16T mineral wagons used previously. *Derek Fear*

# Aftermath

Opposite top: In mid November 1973 the final train of Writhlington coal hauled by No D3169 traverses the level crossing at Radstock West, one of the gates of which appears to have suffered the effects of a collision. The signalman, Ken Evans, keeps a watchful eye on the progress of the train and protects the ungated north side of the crossing from road traffic, the south side gates being intact and effectively barring traffic from that direction. *Derek Fear*

Opposite bottom: D3169 arrives in Radstock West yard ready to handover haulage of the final rake of Writhlington coal to Western class D1028 "Western Hussar". D3169 had entered service in September 1955 and would last in traffic for some 26 years before being withdrawn in July 1982. *Derek Fear*

Above: With the impending departure of the S&D Circle from Radstock in 1975 their stock had to be moved from the shed at Radstock North to the West Somerset Railway. On the 16th. October in that year Class 33 No.33049 makes its way over the level crossing at Radstock West to run over the grass grown track to the spur line connecting the GW line to the S&D. *Derek Fear*

# Aftermath

*Opposite:* Having left S&D metals for the final time and safely reached Radstock West yard the axleboxes of the 2-8-0 are inspected before permission is granted for further transit to the West Somerset Railway. *Derek Fear*

*Above:* Hoisted by crane, provided by the well known firm Sparrows of Bath, onto a low loader on a very wet 23rd. November 1975 the superstructure of the recovered Radstock West signalbox is about to begin its journey by road to Didcot where it will be restored by members of the Great Western Society. *Derek Fear*

Looking rather the worse for wear the former timber superstructure of Radstock West box awaits preservation at Didcot. Today, magnificently restored and mounted on new brick foundations, it has been renamed Radstock North which was its original designation before the neighbouring S&D box took this appellation. Radstock South box features in the view on page 92. It currently houses its original very unusual 5¼ inch spacing of its double twist lever frame which has been relocked to work the layout at Didcot. From the instruments on the block shelf down to the GWR first aid outfit all combine to give an authentic GWR look to the interior of the box. *Derek Fear*

# Somerset & Dorset Demise

Above: In this view Class 33 No. 33109 has arrived at Radstock West yard on 16th. September 1979 with 4TC set No. 417 forming the "Somerset Quarryman" railtour which had somewhat unusually started from Brockenhurst. The tour proceeded to Romsey via Eastleigh and Chandlers Ford and then made its way to Radstock via Westbury and Frome North Junction. It then visited Cranmore before returning to Brockenhurst. It was organised by the British Young Traveller's Society who had also organised the first tour over the closed S&D when No. 77014 visited Blandford Forum on 21st. May 1966. *Derek Fear*

Opposite top: "The Mendipman" railtour organised by F&W Railtours has just arrived at Radstock West yard on 13th. July 1980 with a pair of Class 37s providing the motive power. They were Nos. 37224 and 37233 which had taken over from No. 37138 which had brought the special from Gloucester to Westbury via Hallen Marsh Junction, Avonmouth and Dr. Days Junction. The pair seen above then visited Cranmore before arrival at Radstock. The coaching stock used included a number of TSOs and a BSK Mark 1. *Derek Fear*

Opposite bottom: 3 car DMU unit No. B820 halts at Radstock West yard with the GWS "Devon Rambler" railtour which originated from Cardiff on 11th. October 1980. The tour then ventured far into the West Country by traversing the Yeovil Pen Mill – Junction spur and proceeding to Exeter and Barnstaple before visiting Torrington, Meeth and Meldon Quarry before returning to Cardiff via Bristol. A line of newly refurbished wagons courtesy of the Marcroft Wagon Works can be seen on the right. *Derek Fear*

# Aftermath

# 6
# Erasing the past

Above: The impressive iron train shed at Bath Green Park is seen forty years ago in 1981 just prior to restoration as part of the redevelopment of the site by Sainsbury's supermarket. The roof of the station was designed by the Midland Railway's engineer John Sydney Crossley and was constructed for the sum of £6,086 by Andrew Handyside & Co. iron founders of Derby. The original paint scheme was described as "vermillion, chocolate and white". Following the awarding of a Grade II listing in 1971 and many years of neglect the restored station was formally re-opened on 1 December 1982 by Princess Margaret. The firm of Handyside manufactured everything from cast iron ornaments to bridges producing over 400 of the latter item for the LB&SCR. Other notable trainsheds produced by the firm included those at Glasgow St. Enoch, Bradford Adolphus Street and at Middlesborough. The largest structure built by Handyside, said to be the largest hall in the country covered by one span of iron and glass, was the 1886 National Agricultural Hall in London better known as Olympia. The former warehouse bearing the legend "British Railways (WR) HM Customs & Excise Customs Bonded Store No. 2", which can be seen on the right, was later demolished as part of the redevelopment.

Opposite top: Cyclists and walkers now enjoy traffic free access to the old line, now forming part of Sustrans route 244 known as the Two Tunnels Greenway, as it passes underneath bridge No. 13 Mogers Bridge situated some 1 ¾ miles from Bath Junction and just before the entrance to Combe Down tunnel.

Opposite bottom: The remains of Midford station in this view present a very different appearance to the almost identically positioned shot on page 7 where signalman Wiltshire is wielding his broom. At one time the site of abortive preservation schemes in the mid 1980s and again in the early 1990s planning permission was refused on each occasion. Midford halt's buildings lie destroyed symptomatic of what has happened to the bulk of the infrastructure over this 70 mile route from Bath to Bournemouth in the intervening 55 years since closure. Today the site is far busier than it ever was in railway days as many cyclists and walkers pass the platform here utilising the former trackbed which now forms part of a cycle and pedestrian route. As they pass by many no doubt ponder what it was like when trains still ran over half a century before.

## Somerset & Dorset Demise

# Erasing the past

Opposite top: Taken from the site of the former up sidings in the 1980s this view shows that Evercreech Junction was at the time occupied by a timber yard. Today it houses a number of businesses spread over a much expanded site named the Evecreech Junction Industrial Estate which in its advertising states "Originally opened in 1862 as a busy railway station Evercreech Junction offers over 50 Acres of opportunity." A fascinating drone overfly is available on the website evercreechjunction.co.uk which reveals the extent of the estate and shows the remaining railway infrastructure.

Opposite bottom: This 1988 view taken 22 years after closure reveals that a rotary clothes line adjacent to the coping stones of the former down platform now occupies the site of the erstwhile down line at Evercreech Junction. The space between the tracks has been infilled and apart from the Stationmaster's house and associated buildings on the down side most of the former infrastructure at this important junction has been removed. Today the Stationmaster's house boasts the addition of a conservatory built on the former platform and trackbed.

Above: In this early 1970s view Pylle station building awaits its new role as a dwelling. It too has been subsequently extended to the rear to form an attractive property. I recall the commentary of John Betjeman in his BBC tv film "Let's Imagine a Branch Line Railway" when he said "Take a look at Pylle which was once a station but is now a halt with no one to look after it. I doubt if there's a quieter, sadder sight in Somerset than Pylle when the train has left and it sinks back to silence." Pylle lost its passing loop in 1929, when the 17 lever signalbox was reduced to ground frame status, and the station staff were withdrawn in 1957. The goods yard closed in June 1963 and all tracks removed in early 1967. Silence indeed!

## Somerset & Dorset Demise

West Pennard station still proclaims its previous life although motor vehicles now occupy the erstwhile railway trackbed. The former station master's house appears to be undergoing some rear extension whilst the Goods Shed seen on the right is also undergoing conversion to residential accommodation.

A fitting finale perhaps. As dusk falls on a wet winter's afternoon in December 1967 the dim light from a lamp attached to the footbridge linking the S&D and GW platforms at Highbridge reveals the much rationalised track layout with the former S&D platforms now devoid of buildings. A lone signal lamp on what was formerly platform No. 5 also pierces the gloom and the gaunt remains of Highbridge Works can just be glimpsed in the right background.